IPO INVESTING GUIDE

How to make 100% profit investing in IPO stocks

by
Matthew Smith

© 2021 IPO Investing Guide
By Matthew Smith
All Rights Reserved
Do not share or redistribute without permission.

TABLE OF CONTENTS

Disclaimer..page 3
About the author..page 4

INTRODUCTION... page 5

1. What is the IPO?.. page 7
2. IPO history and statistics............................... page 9
3. Why would a company go public?..................... page 13
4. IPO process. Role of investment bankers......... page 19
5. How to invest money in IPO stocks?................. page 29
6. How to read and analyze the S-1 form?..............page 39
7. Lock up period and hedge strategies...............page 56
8. How to choose the best brokerage service?........page 67
9. IPO Alternatives...page 71
10. IPO ETF and mutual funds............................page 77
11. IPO risks. Invest your money wisely................page 86

CONCLUSION..page 88

Disclaimer

"IPO Investing Guide" is designed for investors with basic knowledge on the stock investing process, stock market, and how to manage the risks.
This guide is designed for educational and entertainment purposes.
The author of "IPO Investing Guide" does not give any recommendation to buy or sell IPOs.
When addressing financial matters in any of my books, I've taken every effort to ensure the accuracy of the information represented and its ability to improve your life or grow your business. However, there is no guarantee that you will get any results or earn any money using any of the ideas, tools, strategies, or recommendations in any part of the content.
Always keep in mind then actual information regarding brokerages, account requirements, commissions, etc. is subject to change. Thus, always do your own research before making a decision to invest money. Nothing in this book is a promise or guarantee of earnings. Your level of success in attaining similar results is dependent upon a number of factors, including your skill, knowledge, ability, dedication, business savvy, network, and financial situation, to name a few.
Because these factors differ according to individuals, I cannot and do not guarantee your success, income level, or ability to earn revenue. You alone are responsible for your actions and results in life and business.
An individual investor should always understand the risks associated with investing in stocks with elevated risk, including IPO.
Always perform your own due diligence before investing money in an IPO. Do not invest money that you cannot afford to lose.

About the author

Matthew Smith is an experienced investor, trader, and entrepreneur. He is a master of IPO, Cryptocurrency, and Venture Investing.
He believes that financial education is essential for modern people. Everyone should invest their time in self-education so everyone can gain their own potential and become financially free or create an additional source of income.
This book will explain how to invest money in profitable IPO stocks and gain capital.
Matthew Smith loves educating and inspiring other entrepreneurs to succeed and live their dreams.

Other books of the author (available on Amazon):

Passive income, a short guide to your financial freedom

Cryptocurrency Investor Handbook

Matthew Smith is on social media!
 Sign up to get information regarding new books released in the investing series!

Facebook Author Page:
https://www.facebook.com/authormatthewsmith

INTRODUCTION

The year 2020 has brought about a lot of surprises: a global pandemic, an economic downturn, millions of jobs lost, and so on. However, it hasn't slowed down the momentum of the initial public offering (IPO) or those looking to profit from IPOs.

2020 was the biggest year ever for IPOs, as well as one of the most innovative years in terms of the increasing reliance on SPACs and direct listings. The U.S. exchanges have accounted for the vast majority of these IPOs, making up 82% of deals and 87% of proceeds in the third quarter of the year, according to the *Global IPO trends: Q3 2020* report published by Dealogic and EY on Oct. 14.
Globally, the third quarter of 2020 was the most active of the past 20 years by proceeds and the second highest third quarter by deal numbers. Analysts found that market liquidity and investor sentiment were key to driving IPO activity last year, with technology, industrials, and health care accounting for 537 IPOs and raising a total of $110.5 billion in 2020.
Some of the most prominent IPOs in 2020 included Casper Sleep Inc. (CSPR), Lemonade, Inc. (LMND), Snowflake Inc. (SNOW), Sumo Logic, Inc. (SUMO), American Well Corporation (AMWL), and Unity Software Inc. (U). In addition, Palantir Technologies Inc. (PLTR) and Asana, Inc. (ASAN) went public via direct listing in September 2020. Array Technologies, Inc. (ARRY), which is the world's second-largest supplier of solar tracking systems, went public in October. Array, based in New Mexico, is the biggest IPO in the state's history.

Overall trends include the rise of the SPAC vehicle, the prominence of cloud-based companies and consumer tech, and a couple of significant companies going public through direct listing this year. The IPO market hasn't been entirely immune to politics: we've also seen several Chinese companies that may have previously listed in the United States flock back to China.

Despite a global pandemic, an election year, and many uncertainties, 2020 was the best IPOs year ever. Airbnb and DoorDash are among the high-profile companies that went public in the fourth quarter.

In the last 2 calendar years alone, 102 different IPOs have given investors a quick double or better.

The best ones produced profits of 864%, 1,021%, and 1,393%.

But if you're like many folks, you may think IPO profits are reserved for multi-millionaire insiders.

You may also think that unless you have insider connections to Wall Street, you're not invited to the party.

Well, there's always been some truth to that... until now.

What I want to share with you is an entirely new way for ordinary investors to profit from IPOs.

Any investor with a few thousand dollars can use this method to start pocketing big potential IPO profits today.

That's important because we're entering what may well be the most lucrative time *ever* for IPOs.

2021 should make the IPO market even stronger. While this trend is keeping on a positive note, you can also become the part of the big IPO game.

This IPO Investing Guide will give you all the answers necessary for you to become an IPO investor and double your income using this trend.

What is the IPO?

So, let's begin with discovering what the IPO actually is.

IPO (Initial Public Offering) or stock market launch is a type of public offering in which the shares of a company are sold to institutional investors and retail (individual) investors. An IPO is underwritten by one or more investment banks, who also arrange for the shares to be listed on one or more stock exchanges. Through this process, colloquially known as *floating* or *going public*, a privately held company is transformed into a public company. Initial public offerings can be used to raise new equity capital for companies, to monetize the investments of private shareholders such as company founders or private equity investors, and to enable the easy trading of existing holdings or future capital raising by becoming publicly traded.

After the IPO, shares are traded freely in the open market at what is known as the free float. Stock exchanges stipulate a minimum free float both in absolute terms (the total value as determined by the share price multiplied by the number of shares sold to the public) and as a proportion of the total share capital (i.e. the number of shares sold to the public divided by the total shares outstanding). Although IPO offers many benefits, there are also significant costs involved – chiefly those associated with the process, such as banking and legal fees, as well as the ongoing requirement to disclose important and sometimes sensitive information.
Initial public offering (IPO) is one type of public offering; not all public offerings are IPOs (I will later explain about other types of public offerings). An IPO occurs only when a company offers its shares (not other securities) for the first time for public ownership and trading, an act making it a public company.

However, public offerings are also made by already-listed companies. The company issues additional securities to the public, adding to those currently being traded. For example, a listed company with 10 million shares outstanding can offer another 5 million shares to the public. This is a public offering, but not an IPO. Once the transaction is complete, the company will have 15 million shares outstanding. Non-initial public offering of equity is also called seasoned equity offering. Other types of securities besides shares can be offered publicly. Bonds, warrants, capital notes, and many other kinds of debt and equity vehicles are offered, issued, and traded in public capital markets. A private company with no shares listed publicly can still issue other securities to the public and have them traded on an exchange. A public company may also offer and list other securities alongside its shares.

Most public offerings are in the primary market – that is, the issuing company itself is the offerer of securities to the public. The offered securities are then issued (allocated) to the new owners. If it is an offering of shares, this means that the company's outstanding capital grows. If it is an offering of other securities, this entails the creation or expansion of a series (of bonds, warrants, etc.). However, more rarely, public offerings take place in the secondary market. This is called a secondary market offering: existing security holders offer to sell their stake to other, new owners, through the stock exchange. The offerer is different from the issuer (the company). A secondary market offering is still a public offering with much the same requirements, including a prospectus.

IPO history and statistics

The earliest form of a company which issued *public shares* was the case of the *publicani* during the Roman Republic. Like modern joint-stock companies, the *publicani* were legal bodies independent of their members whose ownership was divided into shares, or *partes*. There is evidence that these shares were sold to public investors and traded in a type of over-the-counter market in the Forum, near the Temple of Castor and Pollux. The shares fluctuated in value, encouraging the activity of speculators or *quaestors*. Little evidence remains of the prices for which *partes* were sold, the nature of initial public offerings, or a description of stock market behavior. *Publicani* lost favor with the fall of the Republic and the rise of the Empire.

In the early modern period, the Dutch were financial innovators who helped lay the foundations of modern financial systems. The first modern IPO occurred in March 1602, when the Dutch East India Company offered shares of the company to the public in order to raise capital. The Dutch East India Company (VOC) became the first company in history to issue bonds and shares of stock to the general public. In other words, the VOC was officially the first publicly traded company because it was the first company to ever actually be listed on an official stock exchange. While the Italian city-states produced the first transferable government bonds, they did not develop the other ingredient necessary to produce a fully-fledged capital market: corporate shareholders. As Edward Stringham (2015) notes, "companies with transferable shares date back to classical Rome, but these were usually not enduring endeavors and no considerable secondary market existed (Neal, 1997, p. 61)."

In the United States, the first IPO was the public offering of Bank of North America around 1783.

The spring IPO window was cut short by the global pandemic, but as equity markets recovered and volatility normalized, the second half of 2020 saw a revival of the IPO market – particularly in the US and Asia. Notably, the key drivers of the IPO activity in 2020 were Technology, e-commerce, and Health Care IPOs, with a resurgence of SPAC activity in the US. Also, the number of Financial Sponsor IPOs more than doubled in 2020 as compared to the previous year.

Globally, there were 1,415 IPOs in 2020, raising a total of $331.3bn and representing a significant increase from 2019 in terms of the number of transactions and proceeds (2019: 1,040 IPOs raised $199.2bn).
Asia-Pacific accounted for 52% of all global IPO transactions, with 36% in the Americas.

2020 Initial Public Offerings

There were 480 initial public offerings in 2020. October had the most with a total of 97 IPOs. March had the fewest with only 5. View all 2020 IPOs

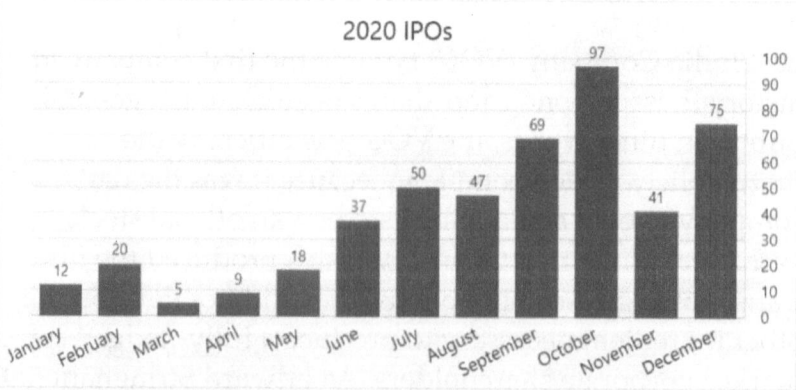

Source: StockAnalysis.com

Notwithstanding the lower number of IPO transactions as compared to Asia-Pacific, the Americas represented 57% ($190.1bn) of global IPO proceeds.

EMEA IPO numbers were up 30% on 2019. However, proceeds were only $0.4bn higher (excluding Saudi Aramco's $25.6bn IPO taking place in Q4 2019).
Global FO numbers were considerably higher than 2019, with 3,689 transactions which raised $734.3bn.
FO activity in the Americas was notably higher in 2020, where 1,484 FOs raised $317.7bn. 2020 FO proceeds in the region were 47% higher ($216.3bn).

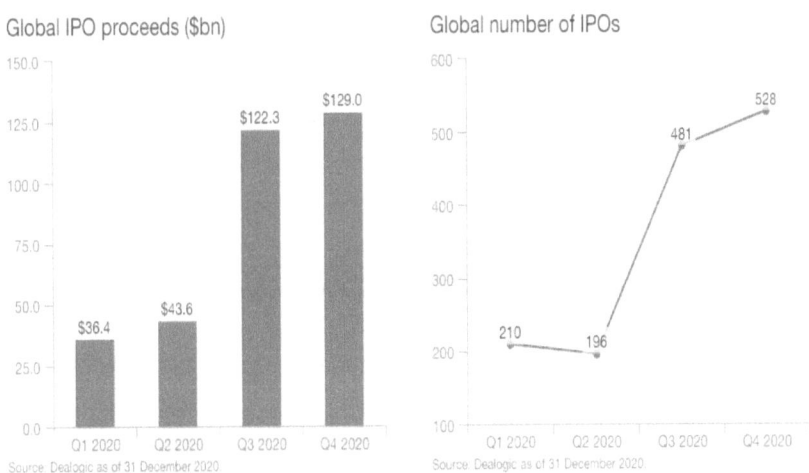

A rollout of COVID-19 vaccines should underpin a global economic recovery in 2021, where corporate earnings can return to pre-pandemic levels. This will build from a position where equity markets have been benefitting from an extended period of low interest rates, low inflation, and government stimulus, particularly in Europe and the US. However, the timing of the expected positive impact on economies, corporate earnings, and capital markets will depend on the progress of immunization programs across the globe.
With strong momentum building in Q3 and Q4 2020, there is a very substantial pipeline of companies looking to IPOs in 2021 in favorable conditions.

The market is expecting more a billion dollar plus IPOs in 2021, including tech unicorns, SPACs, and companies in sectors such as renewables, e-commerce, and healthcare, which are expected to remain attractive for IPO investors. The rising importance of ESG considerations has been further accentuated through the 'build back better' political narrative, which, markets anticipate, will be supported in the positioning of ongoing government support. Investors are increasingly focused on ESG strategy, targets, and performance, while appropriate disclosures in these areas are now seen as prerequisites of a successful IPO, regardless of the industry in which the company operates.

The implications of the change in US political leadership, Brexit, and, more generally, unprecedented government borrowing in response to the pandemic create significant uncertainties for the global economic position as we enter 2021. Arguably, recent investor optimism has increased market vulnerability to any disappointing news and potential negative surprises as the Biden administration takes over in the US, Brexit takes shape, and governments consider how to repair national finances.

Number of IPOs by year

There have been 4,926 IPOs between 2000 and 2021. The most was in the year 2020, with a total of 480 IPOs. The least was in 2009, with only 62 IPOs.

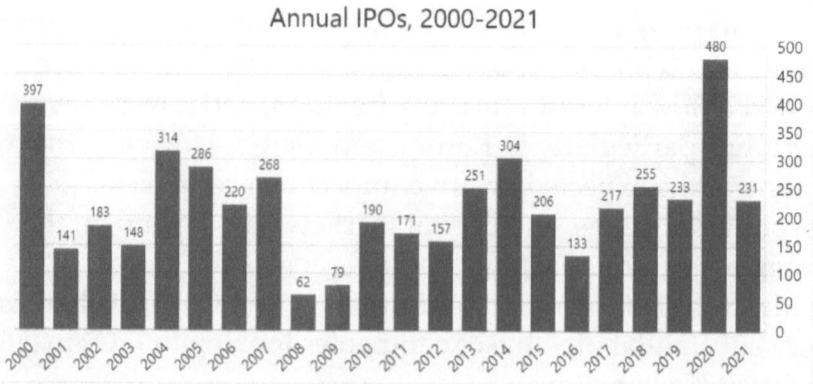

Source: StockAnalysis.com

Why would a company go public?

To get a better understanding of the IPO process, you must know why companies strive to became public.
What is the difference between a private and public company?

A privately held company, private company, or close corporation is a corporation that is owned not by the government or non-governmental organizations, but by a relatively small number of shareholders or company members. It does not offer or trade its company stock (shares) to the general public on the stock market exchanges, but rather the company's stock is offered, owned, and traded or exchanged privately or over-the-counter (OTC or off-exchange trading is done directly between two parties, without the supervision of the exchange). More ambiguous terms for a privately held company are closely held corporation, unquoted company, and unlisted company.

Though less visible than their publicly traded counterparts, private companies have major importance in the world's economy. In 2008, the 441 largest private companies in the United States accounted for US$1,800,000,000,000 ($1.8 trillion) in revenues and employed 6.2 million people, according to *Forbes*. In 2005, using a substantially smaller pool size (22.7%) for comparison, the 339 companies on *Forbes'* survey of closely held U.S. businesses sold a trillion dollars' worth of goods and services (44%) and employed four million people. In 2004, the *Forbes* count of privately held U.S. businesses with at least $1 billion in revenue was 305.

Private ownership of productive assets differs between state ownership or collective ownership (as in worker-owned companies). This usage is often found in former communist countries to differentiate from formerly state-owned enterprises, but it may be used anywhere when contrasting a state-owned or a collectively owned company.

In the United States, the term privately held company is more often used to describe for-profit enterprises whose shares are not traded on the stock market.

In countries with public trading markets, a privately held business is generally taken to mean one whose ownership, shares, or interests are not publicly traded. Often, privately held companies are owned by the company founders or their families and heirs, or by a small group of investors. Sometimes employees also hold shares of private companies.

Most small businesses are privately held.

Subsidiaries and joint ventures of publicly traded companies (for example, General Motors), unless shares in the subsidiary itself are traded directly, have characteristics of both privately held companies and publicly traded companies. Such companies are usually subject to the same reporting requirements as privately held companies, but their assets, liabilities, and activities are also included in the reports of their parent companies, as required by the accountancy and securities industry rules relating to groups of companies.

Private companies may be called corporations, limited companies, limited liability companies, unlimited companies, or other names depending on where and how they are organized and structured. In the United States, but not generally in the United Kingdom, the term is also extended to partnerships, sole proprietorships, or business trusts.

Each of these categories may have additional requirements and restrictions that may impact reporting requirements, income tax liabilities, governmental obligations, employee relations, marketing opportunities, and other business obligations and decisions.

In many countries, there are forms of organization which are restricted to and are commonly used by private companies. For example, the private company limited by shares in the United Kingdom (abbreviated *Ltd*) or unlimited company and the proprietary limited company (abbreviated *Pty Ltd*) or unlimited proprietary company (abbreviated *Pty*) in South Africa and Australia.

A private company can't dip into the public capital markets and must rely on private funding.

While a privately held company can't rely on selling stocks or bonds on the public market in order to raise cash to fund its growth, it may still be able to sell a limited number of shares without registering with the SEC under Regulation D. This way, privately held companies can use shares of equity to attract investors. Of course, privately held companies can also borrow money from either banks or venture capitalists, or rely on profits to fund growth.

The main advantage of private companies is that management doesn't have to answer to stockholders and isn't required to file disclosure statements with the SEC. However, a private company can't dip into the public capital markets and must, therefore, turn to private funding. It has often been said that private companies seek to minimize the tax bite, while public companies seek to increase profits for shareholders.

The popular misconception is that privately held companies are small and of little interest. In fact, there are many big-name companies that are also privately held – check out the *Forbes* list of America's largest private companies, which includes big-name brands like Mars, Cargill, Fidelity Investments, Koch Industries, and Bloomberg.

Public Companies

The main advantage public companies have is their ability to tap the financial markets by selling stock (equity) or bonds (debt) to raise capital (i.e. cash) for expansion and other projects. Bonds are a form of a loan that a publicly held company can take from an investor. It will have to repay this loan with interest, but it won't have to surrender any shares of ownership in the company to the investor. Bonds are a good option for public companies seeking to raise money in a depressed stock market. Stocks, however, allow company founders and owners to liquidate some of their equity in the company, thus relieving growing companies of the burden of repaying bonds.

Key Differences

One of the biggest differences between the two types of companies is how they deal with public disclosure. If it's a public U.S. company, which means it is trading on a U.S. stock exchange, it is typically required to file quarterly earnings reports (among other things) with the Securities and Exchange Commission (SEC). This information is made available to shareholders and the public. Private companies, however, are not required to disclose their financial information to anyone, since they do not trade stock on a stock exchange.
In most cases, a private company is owned by the company's founders, management, or a group of private investors.

A public company is a company that has sold all or a portion of itself to the public via an initial public offering.
Capital can be used to fund research and development (R&D), fund capital expenditure, or even pay off existing debt.

Becoming an IPO is an expensive and time-consuming endeavor; the benefits to going public can be numerous, but so can the drawbacks – especially for smaller businesses. Another advantage is increased public awareness of the company because IPOs often generate publicity by making their products known to a new group of potential customers. Subsequently, this may lead to an increase in market share for the company. An IPO may also be used by founding individuals as an exit strategy. Many venture capitalists have used IPOs to cash in on successful companies that they helped start-up.

The Pros and Cons of a Company Going Public

Even with the benefits of an IPO, public companies often face several disadvantages that may make them think twice about going public. One of the most important changes is the need for added disclosure for investors. In addition, public companies are regulated by the Securities Exchange Act of 1934 in regard to periodic financial reporting, which may be difficult for newer public companies. They must also meet other rules and regulations that are monitored by the Securities and Exchange Commission (SEC).

More importantly, especially for smaller companies, is that the cost of complying with regulatory requirements can be very high. These costs have only increased with the advent of the Sarbanes-Oxley Act. In order to become an IPO, a company must be able to pay for these additional costs, which include the generation of financial reporting documents, audit fees, investor relation departments, and accounting oversight committees.

IPOs often generate publicity by making their products known to a wider potential swath of customers, but taking a company public is a huge risk.

Smaller businesses may find it difficult to afford the time and money it takes to become an IPO.

Privately held companies have more autonomy than public ones.

Public companies are also faced with the added pressure of the market, which may cause them to focus more on short-term results rather than long-term growth. The actions of the company's management also become increasingly scrutinized as investors constantly look for rising profits. This may lead management to use somewhat questionable practices in order to boost earnings.

Before deciding whether or not to go public, companies must evaluate all of the potential advantages and disadvantages that will arise. This usually happens during the underwriting process, as the company works with an investment bank to weigh the pros and cons of a public offering and determine if it's in the best interests of the company for that time period.

IPO process. Role of investment bankers

This chapter will explain the importance of investment bankers, as well as why you should also assess the quality and reputation of underwriters during IPO analytics.

The world of finance is complex. There are many aspects which cannot be fully explained and still confuse researchers. One of the most discussed topics is that of Initial Public Offerings (IPOs), mainly because of the intricate connections between investment bankers (underwriters), issuers, and buyers.

This "IPO Investing Guide" was created to summarize the whole process of going public and emphasize the role of the underwriters. In the "IPO Investing Guide," we mainly discuss the American "way" of going public. However, the procedure is generally the same for the European market with some differences. The advantages, disadvantages, and legal requirements for going public are enlightened in order to understanding the important role the underwriter plays in the whole process. The structure and legal consequences of the due diligence process are presented. The types of agreement between the underwriter and the issuer are described, as well as the consequences that originate from them. The ways to determine the price and advantages and disadvantages of any of these agreements are presented, with respect to the importance of the underwriter's role and liabilities.

The problem with underpricing is discussed in more detail, since this is one of the big challenges in the IPO process. Some theories that explain this phenomenon are briefly discussed, showing the mechanism behind the underpricing problem. Some of the unlawful allocation practices are listed, with examples that show that even the top underwriters use prohibited actions to ensure the successful completion of the IPO process.

The importance of the pre-opening period for the determination of the right market price and the active participation of the underwriter in the bidding during the first day of the offering is emphasized. Finally, we discuss the fact that the reputation of the underwriter is one of the most important qualities that they possess, with respect to the choice of underwriter, the initial returns, and the long-run underperformance of the IPO stocks.

What is the IPO Process?

The Initial Public Offering (IPO) process is where a previously unlisted company sells new or existing securities and offers them to the public for the first time.

Prior to an IPO, a company is considered to be private, with a smaller number of shareholders limited to accredited investors (like angel investors/venture capitalists and high net worth individuals) and/or early investors (for instance the founder, family, and friends).

After an IPO, the issuing company becomes a publicly listed company on a recognized stock exchange. Thus, an IPO is also commonly known as "going public".

Legal Requirements

There are some legal requirements that must be fulfilled when a firm decides to go public.

The most important rules that govern the IPO process are the Securities Act of 1933 (requires the revelation of material information about the securities which will be sold to the public and prohibits the omission or misrepresentation of this material information), the Securities Exchange Act of 1934 (the power of the S.E.C. to register and regulate the participants in the securities market and the right to receive periodic information from publicly traded firms), and the Sarbanes-Oxley Act of 2002 (increases the company responsibility; oversees the activities of the auditing business).

Overview of the IPO Process

This guide will break down the steps involved in the process, which can take anywhere from six months to over a year to complete.

Below are the steps a company must undertake to go public via an IPO process:

1. Select a bank

2. Due diligence and filings
3. Pricing
4. Stabilization
5. Transition

Step 1: Select an investment bank

When a privately held company is gearing up to sell shares to the public, it typically uses Investment Banks to underwrite the IPO or sell the shares on its behalf.
Underwriting an IPO can be very profitable for the banks, which is why competition can be fierce. It's not a guarantee, but an underwriter that has engaged in many IPOs over many years with a good track record is more likely to have a successful offering than a novice Investment Bank that isn't an experienced IPO underwriter.

The first step in the IPO process is for the issuing company to choose an investment bank to advise the company on its IPO and to provide underwriting services. The investment bank is selected according to the following criteria:

- Reputation
- Quality of research
- Industry expertise
- Distribution, i.e. if the investment bank can provide the issued securities to more institutional investors or to more individual investors
- Prior relationship with the investment bank

A firm rarely decides to go public without an intermediate. The intermediate, usually an investment banker (underwriter), facilitates the whole process. The choice of the lead underwriter is a serious task and is done based on several criteria, such as the reputation of the underwriter, their experience in marketing and after-market activities, their knowledge of the market conditions and institutional and retail investors, their experience in the right pricing of the stocks, the experience and quality of the research in the issuer's industry, and the presence of an analyst who can perform an adequate stabilizing policy in the after-market. One of the ways to measure an underwriter's reputation is described in a document from *Cooney Jr., Hill Jr., Jordan, and Singh*.

They use the **ELO** coefficient (the coefficient used in assessing chess players' ratings) in measuring an underwriter's reputation.

The reputation of the underwriter is the most important criteria by which one should be chosen. If their reputation is good and the underwriter is in the *"bulge bracket"* (the top underwriters, according to the measurement of the underwriter's reputation developed by Johnson and Miller), this can further boost the selling of the securities. Also, the better the reputation of the underwriter, the less underpricing is experienced in the short-run. However, it is not only the firm that will choose its investment banker; the process of choosing is a two-way procedure. The underwriters also carefully choose what kind of firm they will represent because of their reputation. If the firm they represent is a risky one and the IPO is not successful, the reputation of the underwriter can be seriously damaged. Usually, firms that raise an IPO of more than 50 million dollars, as well as firms offering unique products which are interesting to the public or companies with capable management, have the chance of signing a *"bulge bracket"* underwriter.

The top 5 IPO underwriters for 2020, ranked by proceeds, are Morgan Stanley, Goldman Sachs, Merrill Lynch, JPMorgan, and Citigroup.

There are two alternatives ways of choosing an investment banker which the issuer can use. The first is called *competitive offer based*, by which the issuer chooses the underwriter who bids the most for the securities. This method is not commonly used since, as was said before, there are many factors other than the proceeds from the issuing which impact the choice. This type of choosing is common only for public utilities companies. The second type is called *negotiated offer based*. With this type of assessing the underwriter, the whole strategy of going public has been considered. The problem with this method is that it is more expensive than the first one.

However, it represents a deal with the underwriter in which the other factors, such as their reputation and ability to attract more investors, are taking the lead in the process of choosing the underwriter. This is the most commonly used method.

Step 2: Due diligence and regulatory filings
Underwriting is the process through which an investment bank (the underwriter) acts as a broker between the issuing company and the investing public to help the issuing company sell its initial set of shares. The following underwriting arrangements are available to the issuing company:
- **Firm Commitment**: Under such an agreement, the underwriter purchases the whole offer and resells the shares to the investing public. The firm commitment underwriting arrangement guarantees the issuing company that a particular sum of money will be raised.

- **Best Efforts Agreement**: Under such an agreement, the underwriter does not guarantee the amount that they will raise for the issuing company. It only sells the securities on behalf of the company.

- **All or None Agreement**: Unless all of the offered shares can be sold, the offering is canceled.

- **Syndicate of Underwriters**: Public offerings can be managed by one underwriter (sole managed) or by multiple managers. When there are multiple managers, one investment bank is selected as the lead or book-running manager. Under such an agreement, the lead investment bank forms a syndicate of underwriters by cementing strategic alliances with other banks, each of which then sells a part of the IPO. Such an agreement arises when the lead investment bank wants to diversify the risk of an IPO among multiple banks.

An underwriter must draft the following documents:

Engagement Letter: A letter of engagement typically includes:
1. Reimbursement clause: This clause mandates that the issuing company must cover all out-of-pocket expenses incurred by the underwriter, even if the IPO is withdrawn during the due diligence stage, the registration stage, or the marketing stage.
2. Gross spread/underwriting discount: Gross spread is arrived at by subtracting the price at which the underwriter purchases the issue from the price at which they sell the issue.

Gross spread = Sale price of the issue sold by the underwriter – Purchase price of the issue bought by the underwriter

Typically, the gross spread is fixed at 7% of the proceeds. The gross spread is used to pay a fee to the underwriter. If there is a syndicate of underwriters, the lead underwriter is paid 20% of the gross spread. 60% of the remaining spread, called "selling concession," is split between the syndicate underwriters in proportion to the number of issues sold by the underwriter. The remaining 20% of the gross spread is used for covering underwriting expenses (for instance, roadshow expenses, underwriting counsel, etc.).

Letter of Intent: A letter of intent typically contains the following information:
1. The underwriter's commitment to enter into an underwriting agreement with the issuing company.
2. A commitment by the issuing company to provide the underwriter with all relevant information and, thus, fully co-operate in all due diligence efforts.
3. An agreement by the issuing company to provide the underwriter with a 15% overallotment option.

The letter of intent does not mention the final offering price.

Underwriting Agreement: The letter of intent remains in effect until the pricing of the securities, after which the underwriting agreement is executed. Thereafter, the underwriter is contractually bound to purchase the issue from the company at a specific price.

Registration Statement: The registration statement consists of information regarding the IPO, the financial statements of the company, the background of the management, insider holdings, any legal problems faced by the company, and the ticker symbol to be used by the issuing company once listed on the stock exchange. The SEC requires that the issuing company and its underwriters file a registration statement after the details of the issue have been agreed upon. The registration statement has two parts:

- **The Prospectus:** This is provided to every investor who buys the issued security.
- **Private Filings:** This is comprised of information which is provided to the SEC for inspection, but is not necessarily made available to the public.

The registration statement ensures that investors have adequate and reliable information about the securities. The SEC then carries out due diligence to ensure that all the required details have been disclosed correctly.

Red Herring Document: In the cooling-off period, the underwriter creates an initial prospectus which consists of the details of the issuing company, save the effective date, and offer price. Once the red herring document has been created, the issuing company and the underwriters market the shares to public investors. Often, underwriters go on roadshows (called dog and pony shows lasting 3 to 4 weeks) to market the shares to institutional investors and evaluate the demand for the shares.

Step 3: Pricing

After the IPO is approved by the SEC, the effective date is decided. On the day before the effective date, the issuing company and the underwriter decide the offer price (i.e. the price at which the shares will be sold by the issuing company) and the precise number of shares to be sold. Deciding the offer price is important because it is the price at which the issuing company raises capital for itself. The following factors affect the offering price:

- The success/failure of the roadshows (as recorded in the order books).
- The company's goal.

- Condition of the market economy.

IPOs are often underpriced to ensure that the issue is fully subscribed/ oversubscribed by the public investors, even if it results in the issuing company not receiving the full value of its shares.

If an IPO is underpriced, the investors of the IPO expect a rise in the price of the shares on the offer day. This increases demand for the issue. Furthermore, underpricing compensates investors for the risk that they taking by investing in the IPO. An offer that is oversubscribed two to three times is considered to be a "good IPO."

Step 4: Stabilization

After the issue has been brought to the market, the underwriter has to provide analyst recommendations, after-market stabilization, and create a market for the stock issued. The underwriter carries out after-market stabilization in the event of order imbalances by purchasing shares at or below the offering price.

Stabilization activities can only be carried out for a short period of time – however, during this period of time, the underwriter has the freedom to trade and influence the price of the issue as prohibitions against price manipulation are suspended.

Step 5: Transition to Market Competition

The final stage of the IPO process, the transition to market competition, starts 25 days after the initial public offering; once the "quiet period" mandated by the SEC ends.

During this period, investors transition from relying on the mandated disclosures and prospectus to relying on the market forces for information regarding their shares. After the 25-day period lapses, underwriters can provide estimates regarding the earning and valuation of the issuing company. Thus, the underwriter assumes the roles of advisor and evaluator once the issue has been made.

Metrics for judging a successful IPO process

The following metrics are used for judging the performance of an IPO:

Market Capitalization: The IPO is considered to be successful if the company's market capitalization is equal to or greater than the market capitalization of industry competitors within 30 days of the initial public offering. Otherwise, the performance of the IPO is in question.

Market Capitalization = Stock Price x Total Number of Company's Outstanding Shares

Market Pricing: The IPO is considered to be successful if the difference between the offering price and the market capitalization of the issuing company 30 days after the IPO is less than 20%. Otherwise, the performance of the IPO is in question.

How to invest money in IPO stocks?

If the goal of investing is to buy low and sell high, then getting in on an initial public offering must be the ticket to riches. Buy a hot new stock at a discount, then sell it for a huge profit just hours or days later, right? Seems like a sure thing.

However, for most individual investors, that dream of getting in on the IPO action will never be realized.

That's not necessarily a bad thing; for every fairy-tale stock that takes off like a rocket following an IPO, there are cautionary tales of plenty of IPOs that post lackluster results. Some – such as meal delivery service Blue Apron – even crash and burn.

Even during the COVID-19 pandemic, there have been a number of long-awaited IPOs with big names such as Airbnb, Snowflake, and Door Dash hitting the market.

However, before rushing to invest a pocketful of cash in an IPO, it's important to know how to buy an IPO and what restrictions you will meet on the way.

That's why I wrote this "IPO Investing Guide" – so you have the opportunity to find the best IPO deals on the market and make money.

The goal of an IPO in the first place is to raise a certain amount of capital for the company to run its business. Thus, selling a million shares to an institutional investor is much more efficient than finding 1,000 individuals to purchase the same amount.

But even big institutions often don't get as much of the action as they would like, because the initial public offering sells only a limited number of shares.

"Especially with a smaller IPO, nobody really gets 100 percent of their fill. In fact, no one gets more than 10 percent of their interest in the allocation," says Kathleen Shelton Smith, principal at Renaissance Capital, a global IPO and investment adviser.

Who gets to buy IPO stocks?

Institutions that get to participate in the initial public offering often do a lot of business with the brokers underwriting the deal.

It's stacked in favor of large asset managers, but it's a money game and everyone is in it to make a buck. That's where [the stock] goes — to the best customers of those brokers.

The reality is your broker perceives individual investors as poor. Instead, management, employees, friends, and families of the company going public may be offered the chance to buy shares at the IPO price in addition to investment banks, hedge funds, and institutions. High-net-worth clients may be rewarded with IPO shares from time-to-time as well.

If you have an account with the broker bringing the company public and happen to keep most of your vast fortune with that broker, you may be able to beg your way into a hot IPO.

Opportunities don't come easy and there are no guarantees. Even if you manage to gain access to an IPO, the allocation may never come through. Other times, the companies available are low-quality from the start and profits never materialize.

Some IPOs are a huge success, meaning IPO investors can make quick profits or continue investing for the long-term. These are the opportunities we want to find. To access and profit from IPOs, you will need to have your own plan and strategy – then follow it. With experience, you can always amend or change your plan.

Usually I divide all IPO investing process into 5 sections:

1. Analyze the companies intending to go public.
2. Get access to an IPO.
3. Action - before, during, and after an IPO, you'll need to take action to gain access and receive allocation.
4. Receive a stock allocation from an IPO before the trading starts.

5. Exit plan – after you receive allocation and trading starts, you are the owner of the allocated stocks. Thus, you must have to decide whether to sell the stocks after the Lock Up period, before this period, or to keep them long-term.

Let's dip further into each of the above sections.

Analyze the company

You should first perform broad IPO market analyses and pipeline.

The IPO market is strongest when the broader stock markets are healthy and uncertainty is low. The best conditions are usually during a bull market, when economic growth is positive. IPO market health can also be judged by the success of other recent IPOs, particularly in the same sector. If a similar company recently launched an IPO, other companies in the same industries will often follow.
Geopolitical events, international conflicts, elections, and Federal Reserve activity also play a role.
IPO investors should be constantly following the IPO news, pipeline, and company filings.
Not all filings are relevant. Some filings are called "blank check" filings, meaning the company is not well established, but still aiming to fund itself through an IPO (later on we will talk closely about "blank check" companies).

List the most relevant IPOs you can find on IPO websites such as IPO Boutique and Renaissance Capital.

Next step is to perform S-1 form analysis.

If you want analyze a company you can use Yahoo Finance, Simply Wall Street, or another web resource. However, normal online research tools such as Yahoo Finance, Morningstar, or a brokerage research center won't work with IPO stocks because the information isn't yet available there. That's because the information you need is only in the SEC filing. For Reg A+ IPOs, it's called Form 1-A. Some foreign IPOs filing in the U.S. are registered as Form F-1. The S-1 is the first formal filing required by the SEC for any company aiming to trade publicly. This document follows a consistent format throughout.

The document includes basic business information, underwriters, planned funding amounts, share data, financials, and company risks. This document is sometimes accompanied by an investor presentation shared with investors leading up to the IPO. The investor presentation is a more reader-friendly PowerPoint presentation with nice photographs, charts, summaries, and data on the company's market opportunity. The S-1 is the primary document for all IPO investors to study, but it's not the only evaluation.

It should be noted that S-1 filings can be made confidentially if a company's annual revenue is less than $1 billion. However, as the IPO approaches, the filing is made public weeks before the offering.

In the next chapter, we will look more closely about S-1 form analysis.

The last step is about IPO demand and hype.
Due diligence and traditional valuation metrics are critical for learning how to invest in IPOs. However, there's a third component that is less quantitative: demand.

Demand for IPOs is difficult to measure as an ordinary investor. The basic idea is you want to determine whether investors like the company and pricing – or not.

Price range is one factor to consider when making this determination. The IPO price range is disclosed in the IPO prospectus and usually via your broker. The range is usually about $2-3 USD. For example, the underwriters might price the range from $14-16.

The night before the IPO starts to trade, the underwriters announce the final pricing. If the final price is at the high end or higher than the range, it's a sign of good demand. Low or below the range means bad demand.

When demand is on the high end, the IPO often increases in value when the stock begins to trade. If demand is low, the offering will be flat or down.

However, if a deal is priced too high, investors may be less likely to buy the deal. This was the case with Facebook; underwriters priced the deal too high and the stock subsequently fell for a period after.

The opposite was true with the Square IPO. The pricing by the underwriter was disappointing to selling investors (venture capital, employees, etc.) as it was priced below the range at $9. Investors with access, on the other hand, rejoiced when the stock jumped up 45% on the first day of trading.

Pricing the deal plays an important role. However, only the underwriters and their connections have a view into this window. Individuals need to judge demand by utilizing publicly available resources and reading as much as possible about the deal. This includes, but is not limited to, sites such as Seeking Alpha, Bloomberg, The Motley Fool, and The Wall Street Journal.

Other less reputable sources include the hashtags of Twitter and various trading forums around the Internet. The more media coverage and household knowledge of a company, the higher the early trading often goes.

As someone who invests completely independently of Wall Street and the securities industry, it seems the best way to learn about IPO demand is to know someone working at the company or as an underwriter. Often, those with knowledge of the deal share information on Twitter or elsewhere, without, it is assumed, violating any insider trading or securities regulations.

Questions You Need to Answer Beforehand

Is It Really the Best IPO?

There are certain questions you need to ask before investing in an IPO. These questions help you to determine the potential of an IPO.

Accordingly, consider the following:

Is the Company Stable?

Here's the part where you need to fall back on the company's prospectus. It'll give you an idea of whether it is stable based on its revenue and earnings over the past few years. Thus, consider whether your investment will be going into a growing company or one that's struggling.

How Much are the Stocks Worth?

The price of a company's stock when it hits the market is an important factor to consider. The price range at which these stocks will be sold may be disclosed by the company in its prospectus. The latter is often revised when the IPO is close. Aside from the price, it's also useful to consider the valuation of the company.

Do Management Have Shares?

The company's prospectus reveals the payment system set up for the management. Professional investors often settle for IPOs from companies whose management has a larger holding of the stock. This is evidence that management is a firm believer in the company's future.

What Will the Cash be Used For?

What purpose will your money, as well as that gathered from other investors, be put to? That's another question to ask. Good use of the raised funds is in an area such as expansion instead of paying private investors who want to sell their shares.

Then you need to get access to IPO investing

Some online brokerages provide IPO access to their customers. However, not all customers are considered equal. Traditional brokers that have relationships with large investment banks often receive IPO shares to distribute to customers. Because of the overwhelming demand for some IPOs, not all customers can get access. The shares of high-demand IPOs go to the wealthiest customers first, then other customers may get access if any shares are leftover.

Brokers and underwriters have pre-existing relationships that dictate share distributions. To shrink the pool of investors, the brokers require account minimums to be eligible. For example, TD Ameritrade requires a $250,000 minimum account balance or 30+ trades in the past three months.

Other brokers such as ETRADE claim to offer access to everyone. However, low account balance customers are unlikely to receive an allocation for a high-demand IPO.

If your account balance is below the stated threshold, you won't get access from a full-service online broker. Even if you meet the minimum balance, the hot IPOs are difficult to access. You'll need an account balance higher than the minimum.

Most brokers give preference to their highest-value customers. If that's not you, you'll need to find other sources of access.
In the separate chapter I'll give you more detailed information regarding the best brokers that offer access to IPOs.

Next step is action
If you do find access to a hot deal, you'll need to act quickly or you'll miss out.
Brokers use email to inform eligible investors when an IPO opportunity is live. For most, having an account is not enough; you'll need to be on the IPO interest email list as well. Check with your broker to see if they offer IPOs and find out how to learn about upcoming deals.
When you receive an email inviting you to participate in an interesting deal, quickly respond to reserve your shares. Give yourself an advantage by implementing email alerts on your smartphone when they come from your broker.
Once you've made a reservation, you can then proceed to completing your due diligence and deciding whether or not you want to invest. You can back out by either withdrawing your reservation or by failing to fund your allocation. No funds, no shares.
The evening before an IPO begins trading on an exchange, underwriters price the deal. If the deal is within their price range, investors can sit tight and wait for their allocation. When the pricing is outside of your range, you'll need to pay attention to communication coming from your broker. In this event, you may need to confirm your reservation request before receiving an allocation. Brokers use both email and text messages to confirm a reservation.

Now we're waiting for our allocation
Investors who successfully participate in an IPO are rewarded with an allocation.

The allocations are distributed after the pricing of the deal. Pricings usually take place after the market closing the night before an IPO, with the allocations to follow.

The allocation is the physical placement of the shares into your brokerage account. You may receive all or a fraction of the shares requested, depending on how many shares are available through your broker and deal-wide. An email typically follows to inform you of the allocation amount.

If you're investing via escrow, which is common on some sites such as BANQ, it may be a day or two before the shares are delivered. For Motif, TD Ameritrade, Fidelity, and other large online brokers, it's done in real-time.

Your allocation will show in your brokerage account. Once the stock begins trading on the exchange, you are free to hold or sell like any other holding.

Reservations aren't always fulfilled.

The last step of IPO investing is to always have an exit plan

Once you receive an allocation in your brokerage account and the stock begins trading, it's like any other stock.

You have to decide what you will do with the stocks that were allocated to you. You can sell them after trading starts, wait until completion of the lock-up period, or even keep them for much longer if you trust in the company and the future of their business.

How to read and analyze the S-1 form?

What is SEC Form S-1?
SEC Form S-1 is the initial registration form for new securities required by the SEC for public companies that are based in the U.S. Any security that meets the criteria must have an S-1 filing before shares can be listed on a national exchange, such as the New York Stock Exchange. Companies usually file SEC Form S-1 in anticipation of their initial public offering (IPO). Form S-1 requires companies to provide information on the planned use of capital proceeds, detail the current business model and competition, and provide a brief prospectus of the planned security itself, offering price methodology and any dilution that will occur to other listed securities.

SEC Form S-1 is also known as the registration statement under the Securities Act of 1933. Additionally, the SEC requires the disclosure of any material business dealings between the company and its directors and outside counsel. Investors can view S-1 filings online to perform due diligence on new offerings prior to their issue.

If any foreign companies issue securities in the U.S., they are not required to use Form S-1, but instead must fill out SEC Form F-1.

Form S-1 has two parts. Part I, which is also called the prospectus, is a legal document that requires information on the following: business operations, the use of proceeds, total proceeds, the price per share, a description of management, financial condition, the percentage of the business being sold by individual holders, and information on the underwriters. Part II is not legally required in the prospectus. This part includes recent sales of unregistered securities, exhibits, and financial statement schedules. The issuer will have liability if there are material misrepresentations or omissions.
The form is sometimes amended as material information changes or general market conditions cause a delay in the offering. In this case, the issuer needs to file Form S-1/A. The Securities Exchange Act of 1933, often referred to as the Truth in Securities law, requires that these registration forms be filed to disclose important information upon registration of a company's securities. This helps the SEC achieve the Act's objectives: requiring investors to receive significant information regarding securities offered and prohibit fraud in the sale of the offered securities.

Where to Find S-1 Filings
Now that we know we want to read S-1 filings, where do we get them? It's time you get familiar with our friend Edgar.

Edgar isn't a grumpy accountant down the hallway. Instead, it's an SEC service you can access for free. What we want is this particular Edgar search function that lets us hunt for company-specific filings.

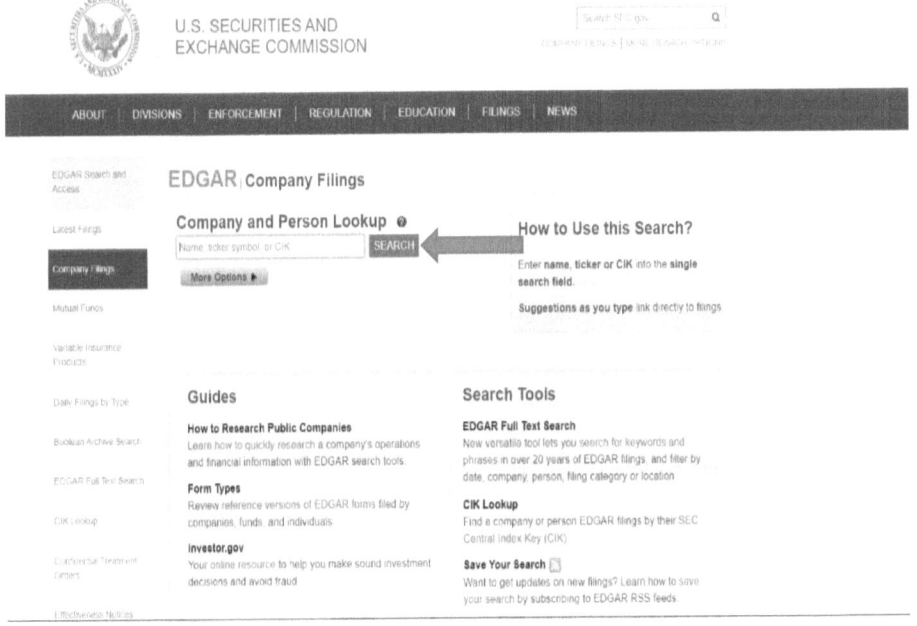

In the search bar, just type in the name of company, which Form S-1 are you looking for, and click search.

Once you've clicked on the right company, you will land on a page with a list of filings. The filing you're looking for will be listed as "S-1."

You may see two forms – S-1 and S-1/A filings. An S-1/A is an amended S-1 filing. A company going public may file an S-1/A if it needs to include more information – for instance, an S-1/A could include an additional quarter of financial details. However, what we want first is the S-1.

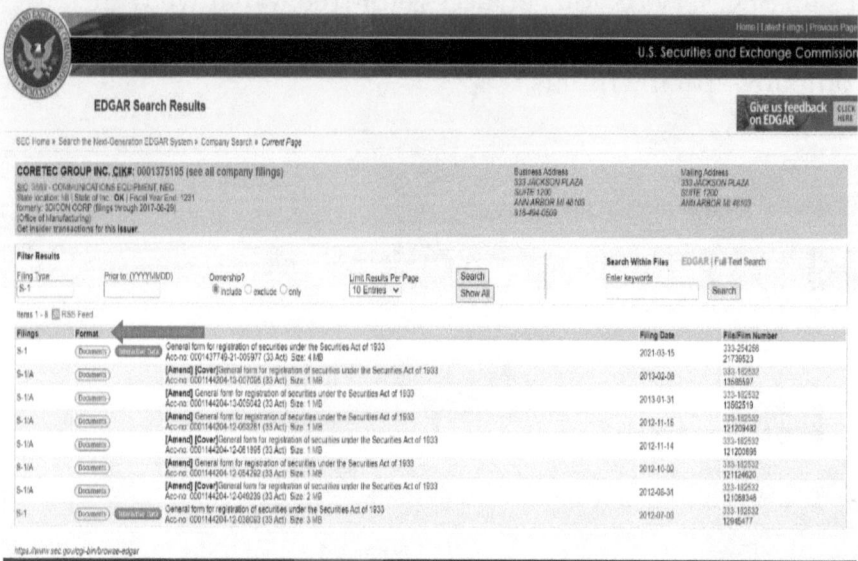

Now that we know where an S-1 filing can be found, we will start with the financial bits, talk about how to size an offering, peek at how companies describe themselves, and chat risks. First, however, let's take a look about the basics, which contain S-1 filing. If I go over every detail and nuance of an S-1, then this book will be about the S-1 Form and not about IPOs. If you want to learn every nuance and detail, use your own curiosity and Google for financial jargon.

Analyzing an S-1, we will get:

- How much money comes in the door (revenue).
- How much the money coming through the door costs (cost of revenue).
- How much the company spends to run (operating costs).
- How much or how little money is left after we subtract costs (profit).

To get this information, you will need to take a look at a company's income statement. Think of this statement as a filter. Up top is the revenue. From there, we'll begin to take costs into account. If any revenue makes it all the way to the bottom of the filter after each cost is accounted for, what's left over is profit. If the company runs out of revenue while paying costs, the deficit it reports is its loss.

Note that everything is in thousands, so if a line says $1,000 it means $1,000,000!

	Year Ended December 31,			Three Months Ended March 31,	
	2015	2016	2017	2017	2018
	(in thousands, except per share data)				
Consolidated Statements of Operations Data:					
Revenue(1)	$ 93,466	$ 124,371	$ 187,727	$ 40,481	$ 59,107
Cost of revenue(2)	10,914	14,219	25,588	4,438	8,728
Gross profit	82,552	110,152	162,139	36,043	50,379
Operating expenses:					
Sales and marketing(1)(2)	60,635	85,736	116,299	26,168	39,588
Research and development(2)	25,288	40,085	57,673	12,458	17,185
General and administrative(2)	15,348	20,164	28,927	6,163	9,055
Recapitalization costs(3)	67,039	—	—	—	—
Total operating expenses	168,310	145,985	202,899	44,789	65,828
Loss from operations	(85,758)	(35,833)	(40,760)	(8,746)	(15,449)
Other expense, net	189	532	91	29	8
Loss before income taxes	(85,947)	(36,365)	(40,851)	(8,775)	(15,457)
(Benefit from) provision for income taxes	(2,188)	843	171	51	431
Net loss	(83,759)	(37,208)	(41,022)	(8,826)	(15,888)
Accretion of Series A and B redeemable convertible preferred stock	29	763	763	187	188
Net loss attributable to common stockholders	$ (83,788)	$ (37,971)	$ (41,785)	$ (9,013)	$ (16,076)
Net loss per share attributable to common stockholders, basic and diluted(4)	$ (1.45)	$ (1.81)	$ (1.88)	$ (0.42)	$ (0.68)
Weighted-average shares used to compute net loss per share attributable to common stockholders, basic and diluted	57,654	20,974	22,211	21,257	23,495
Pro forma net loss per share, basic and diluted (unaudited)(5)			$ (0.53)		$ (0.20)
Weighted-average shares used in computing pro forma net loss per share, basic and diluted (unaudited)			77,597		78,881

In an income statement, each column corresponds to a different time period. The first column is the year ending December 31, 2015, the column to its right is the same period in 2016, and the next is the same period in 2017. Finally, on the far right, we have two columns that describe a three-month period (one quarter) in both 2017 and 2018.

Why do companies include single-quarter results in addition to yearly results? It helps investors zoom in on the firm's most recent performance. By providing the March 31 quarter's results from both 2018 and 2017, we can see how much the company grew from the first quarter of 2017 to the first quarter of 2018. As a result, you can make year-over-year comparisons of the company's first quarters from the last two years.

Now look at the far-right column. We are going to peek at the March 31, 2018 quarter.

Here's Revenue: $59.1 million

Comparing this figure to the number directly to its left (the March 31, 2017 quarter's revenue), we can see that company grew from the quarter of a year ago. That's good. Companies want to grow fast. The faster a company grows, the more valuable it tends to be.

IPO Investing Guide

	Year Ended December 31,			Three Months Ended March 31,	
	2015	2016	2017	2017	2018
	(in thousands, except per share data)				
Consolidated Statements of Operations Data:					
Revenue(1)	$ 93,466	$ 124,371	$ 187,727	$ 40,481	59,107
Cost of revenue(2)	10,914	14,219	25,588	4,438	8,728
Gross profit	82,552	110,152	162,139	36,043	50,379
Operating expenses:					
Sales and marketing(1)(2)	60,635	85,736	116,299	26,168	39,588
Research and development(2)	25,288	40,085	57,673	12,458	17,185
General and administrative(2)	15,348	20,164	28,927	6,163	9,055
Recapitalization costs(3)	67,039	—	—	—	—
Total operating expenses	168,310	145,985	202,899	44,789	65,828
Loss from operations	(85,758)	(35,833)	(40,760)	(8,746)	(15,449)
Other expense, net	189	532	91	29	8
Loss before income taxes	(85,947)	(36,365)	(40,851)	(8,775)	(15,457)
(Benefit from) provision for income taxes	(2,188)	843	171	51	431
Net loss	(83,759)	(37,208)	(41,022)	(8,826)	(15,888)
Accretion of Series A and B redeemable convertible preferred stock	29	763	763	187	188
Net loss attributable to common stockholders	$ (83,788)	$ (37,971)	$ (41,785)	$ (9,013)	$ (16,076)
Net loss per share attributable to common stockholders, basic and diluted(4)	$ (1.45)	$ (1.81)	$ (1.88)	$ (0.42)	$ (0.68)
Weighted-average shares used to compute net loss per share attributable to common stockholders, basic and diluted	57,654	20,974	22,211	21,257	23,495
Pro forma net loss per share, basic and diluted (unaudited)(5)			$ (0.53)		$ (0.20)
Weighted-average shares used in computing pro forma net loss per share, basic and diluted (unaudited)			77,597		78,881

Cost of revenue: $8.7 million

This is the first cost that we'll use to begin filtering revenue to see if the company made any money. Cost of revenue, also called Cost of Goods Sold (COGS), deals with direct costs relating to revenue. For a cloud company, this is the Amazon Web Services bill generated by hosting their service. For Boeing, it would be the titanium and aluminum that goes into making a plane.

	Year Ended December 31,			Three Months Ended March 31,	
	2015	2016	2017	2017	2018
	(In thousands, except per share data)				
Consolidated Statements of Operations Data:					
Revenue(1)	$ 93,466	$ 124,371	$ 187,727	$ 40,481	59,107
Cost of revenue(2)	10,914	14,219	25,588	4,438	8,728
Gross profit	82,552	110,152	162,139	36,043	50,379
Operating expenses:					
Sales and marketing(1)(2)	60,635	85,736	116,299	26,168	39,588
Research and development(2)	25,288	40,085	57,673	12,458	17,185
General and administrative(2)	15,348	20,164	28,927	6,163	9,055
Recapitalization costs(3)	67,039	—	—	—	—
Total operating expenses	168,310	145,985	202,899	44,789	65,828
Loss from operations	(85,758)	(35,833)	(40,760)	(8,746)	(15,449)
Other expense, net	189	532	91	29	8
Loss before income taxes	(85,947)	(36,365)	(40,851)	(8,775)	(15,457)
(Benefit from) provision for income taxes	(2,188)	843	171	51	431
Net loss	(83,759)	(37,208)	(41,022)	(8,826)	(15,888)
Accretion of Series A and B redeemable convertible preferred stock	29	763	763	187	188
Net loss attributable to common stockholders	$ (83,788)	$ (37,971)	$ (41,785)	$ (9,013)	$ (16,076)
Net loss per share attributable to common stockholders, basic and diluted(4)	$ (1.45)	$ (1.81)	$ (1.88)	$ (0.42)	$ (0.68)
Weighted-average shares used to compute net loss per share attributable to common stockholders, basic and diluted	57,654	20,974	22,211	21,257	23,495
Pro forma net loss per share, basic and diluted (unaudited)(5)			$ (0.53)		$ (0.20)
Weighted-average shares used in computing pro forma net loss per share, basic and diluted (unaudited)			77,597		78,881

Gross profit: $50.4 million

Here we have the loosest of profit metrics. Revenue minus cost of revenue equals gross profit. This is not the sort of profitability that most people mean when they discuss the concept. Instead, gross tells us how much revenue the firm in question has left after paying for revenue inputs to run its business. In overly simplified terms, if a company has operating expenses lower than its gross profit, the firm will generate profit in the sense that most people mean it.

	Year Ended December 31,			Three Months Ended March 31,	
	2015	2016	2017	2017	2018
	(in thousands, except per share data)				
Consolidated Statements of Operations Data:					
Revenue(1)	$ 93,466	$ 124,371	$ 187,727	$ 40,481	$ 59,107
Cost of revenue(2)	10,914	14,219	25,588	4,438	8,728
Gross profit	82,552	110,152	162,139	36,043	50,379
Operating expenses:					
Sales and marketing(1)(2)	60,635	85,736	116,299	26,168	39,588
Research and development(2)	25,288	40,085	57,673	12,458	17,185
General and administrative(2)	15,348	20,164	28,927	6,163	9,055
Recapitalization costs(3)	67,039	—	—	—	—
Total operating expenses	168,310	145,985	202,899	44,789	65,828
Loss from operations	(85,758)	(35,833)	(40,760)	(8,746)	(15,449)
Other expense, net	189	532	91	29	8
Loss before income taxes	(85,947)	(36,365)	(40,851)	(8,775)	(15,457)
(Benefit from) provision for income taxes	(2,188)	843	171	51	431
Net loss	(83,759)	(37,208)	(41,022)	(8,826)	(15,888)
Accretion of Series A and B redeemable convertible preferred stock	29	763	763	187	188
Net loss attributable to common stockholders	$ (83,788)	$ (37,971)	$ (41,785)	$ (9,013)	$ (16,076)
Net loss per share attributable to common stockholders, basic and diluted(4)	$ (1.45)	$ (1.81)	$ (1.88)	$ (0.42)	$ (0.68)
Weighted-average shares used to compute net loss per share attributable to common stockholders, basic and diluted	57,654	20,974	22,211	21,257	23,495
Pro forma net loss per share, basic and diluted (unaudited)(5)			$ (0.53)		$ (0.20)
Weighted-average shares used in computing pro forma net loss per share, basic and diluted (unaudited)			77,597		78,881

Operating expenses: $65.8 million

Next in the list is a company's various operating expenses, including sales and marketing costs, research costs, general and administrative expenses, and the like. These add together to create the "Operating expenses" line item. Think of these costs as the expenses that run the company. This is salaries, catered lunches, different meetings, paying sales commissions, and share-based compensation costs.

	Year Ended December 31,			Three Months Ended March 31,	
	2015	2016	2017	2017	2018
	(in thousands, except per share data)				
Consolidated Statements of Operations Data:					
Revenue(1)	$ 93,466	$ 124,371	$ 187,727	$ 40,481	$ 59,107
Cost of revenue(2)	10,914	14,219	25,588	4,438	8,728
Gross profit	82,552	110,152	162,139	36,043	50,379
Operating expenses:					
Sales and marketing(1)(2)	60,635	85,736	116,299	26,168	39,588
Research and development(2)	25,288	40,085	57,673	12,458	17,185
General and administrative(2)	15,348	20,164	28,927	6,163	9,055
Recapitalization costs(3)	67,039	—	—	—	—
Total operating expenses	168,310	145,985	202,899	44,789	65,828
Loss from operations	(85,758)	(35,833)	(40,760)	(8,746)	(15,449)
Other expense, net	189	532	91	29	8
Loss before income taxes	(85,947)	(36,365)	(40,851)	(8,775)	(15,457)
(Benefit from) provision for income taxes	(2,188)	843	171	51	431
Net loss	(83,759)	(37,208)	(41,022)	(8,826)	(15,888)
Accretion of Series A and B redeemable convertible preferred stock	29	763	763	187	188
Net loss attributable to common stockholders	$ (83,788)	$ (37,971)	$ (41,785)	$ (9,013)	$ (16,076)
Net loss per share attributable to common stockholders, basic and diluted(4)	$ (1.45)	$ (1.81)	$ (1.88)	$ (0.42)	$ (0.68)
Weighted-average shares used to compute net loss per share attributable to common stockholders, basic and diluted	57,654	20,974	22,211	21,257	23,495
Pro forma net loss per share, basic and diluted (unaudited)(5)			$ (0.53)		$ (0.20)
Weighted-average shares used in computing pro forma net loss per share, basic and diluted (unaudited)			77,597		78,881

Loss from operations: $15.4 million

Recall when we said that if a firm's operating costs are smaller than its gross profit, it will (generally) make money? Well, if we look at our numbers from the preceding two paragraphs, what do we see? The opposite. So, when we subtract operating expenses ($65.828 million) from gross profit ($50.379 million), we find that our filter has already run out of revenue and has created a hole of $15.4 million.

	Year Ended December 31,			Three Months Ended March 31,	
	2015	2016	2017	2017	2018
	(in thousands, except per share data)				
Consolidated Statements of Operations Data:					
Revenue(1)	$ 93,466	$ 124,371	$ 187,727	$ 40,481	$ 59,107
Cost of revenue(2)	10,914	14,219	25,588	4,438	8,728
Gross profit	82,552	110,152	162,139	36,043	50,379
Operating expenses:					
Sales and marketing(1)(2)	60,635	85,736	116,299	26,168	39,588
Research and development(2)	25,288	40,085	57,673	12,458	17,185
General and administrative(2)	15,348	20,164	28,927	6,163	9,055
Recapitalization costs(3)	67,039	—	—	—	—
Total operating expenses	168,310	145,985	202,899	44,789	65,828
Loss from operations	(85,758)	(35,833)	(40,760)	(8,746)	(15,449)
Other expense, net	189	532	91	29	8
Loss before income taxes	(85,947)	(36,365)	(40,851)	(8,775)	(15,457)
(Benefit from) provision for income taxes	(2,188)	843	171	51	431
Net loss	(83,759)	(37,208)	(41,022)	(8,826)	(15,888)
Accretion of Series A and B redeemable convertible preferred stock	29	763	763	187	188
Net loss attributable to common stockholders	$ (83,788)	$ (37,971)	$ (41,785)	$ (9,013)	$ (16,076)
Net loss per share attributable to common stockholders, basic and diluted(4)	$ (1.45)	$ (1.81)	$ (1.88)	$ (0.42)	$ (0.68)
Weighted-average shares used to compute net loss per share attributable to common stockholders, basic and diluted	57,654	20,974	22,211	21,257	23,495
Pro forma net loss per share, basic and diluted (unaudited)(5)			$ (0.53)		$ (0.20)
Weighted-average shares used in computing pro forma net loss per share, basic and diluted (unaudited)			77,597		78,881

Other expenses, net: $8,000

Every business is distinct and companies often have some other costs that don't fit into their operating results. Those costs could end up on this line. What this figure lets us do is understand the difference between a company's operating results (its operating profit or loss) and its net profit or loss.

	Year Ended December 31,			Three Months Ended March 31,	
	2015	2016	2017	2017	2018
	(in thousands, except per share data)				
Consolidated Statements of Operations Data:					
Revenue(1)	$ 93,466	$ 124,371	$ 187,727	$ 40,481	$ 59,107
Cost of revenue(2)	10,914	14,219	25,588	4,438	8,728
Gross profit	82,552	110,152	162,139	36,043	50,379
Operating expenses:					
Sales and marketing(1)(2)	60,635	85,736	116,299	26,168	39,588
Research and development(2)	25,288	40,085	57,673	12,458	17,185
General and administrative(2)	15,348	20,164	28,927	6,163	9,055
Recapitalization costs(3)	67,039	—	—	—	—
Total operating expenses	168,310	145,985	202,899	44,789	65,828
Loss from operations	(85,758)	(35,833)	(40,760)	(8,746)	(15,449)
Other expense, net	189	532	91	29	8
Loss before income taxes	(85,947)	(36,365)	(40,851)	(8,775)	(15,457)
(Benefit from) provision for income taxes	(2,188)	843	171	51	431
Net loss	(83,759)	(37,208)	(41,022)	(8,826)	(15,888)
Accretion of Series A and B redeemable convertible preferred stock	29	763	763	187	188
Net loss attributable to common stockholders	$ (83,788)	$ (37,971)	$ (41,785)	$ (9,013)	$ (16,076)
Net loss per share attributable to common stockholders, basic and diluted(4)	$ (1.45)	$ (1.81)	$ (1.88)	$ (0.42)	$ (0.68)
Weighted-average shares used to compute net loss per share attributable to common stockholders, basic and diluted	57,654	20,974	22,211	21,257	23,495
Pro forma net loss per share, basic and diluted (unaudited)(5)			$ (0.53)		$ (0.20)
Weighted-average shares used in computing pro forma net loss per share, basic and diluted (unaudited)			77,597		78,881

Net loss: $15.9 million

This is the number that we're looking for. Net loss is what we get after all the company's costs have been removed from revenue. In this case, as we expected, the company lost money as its gross profit wasn't enough to cover its operating expenses, let alone its other costs.

	Year Ended December 31,			Three Months Ended March 31,	
	2015	2016	2017	2017	2018
	(in thousands, except per share data)				
Consolidated Statements of Operations Data:					
Revenue(1)	$ 93,466	$ 124,371	$ 187,727	$ 40,481	$ 59,107
Cost of revenue(2)	10,914	14,219	25,588	4,438	8,728
Gross profit	82,552	110,152	162,139	36,043	50,379
Operating expenses:					
Sales and marketing(1)(2)	60,635	85,736	116,299	26,168	39,588
Research and development(2)	25,288	40,085	57,673	12,458	17,185
General and administrative(2)	15,348	20,164	28,927	6,163	9,055
Recapitalization costs(3)	67,039	—	—	—	—
Total operating expenses	168,310	145,985	202,899	44,789	65,828
Loss from operations	(85,758)	(35,833)	(40,760)	(8,746)	(15,449)
Other expense, net	189	532	91	29	8
Loss before income taxes	(85,947)	(36,365)	(40,851)	(8,775)	(15,457)
(Benefit from) provision for income taxes	(2,188)	843	171	51	431
Net loss	(83,759)	(37,208)	(41,022)	(8,826)	(15,888)
Accretion of Series A and B redeemable convertible preferred stock	29	763	763	187	188
Net loss attributable to common stockholders	$ (83,788)	$ (37,971)	$ (41,785)	$ (9,013)	$ (16,076)
Net loss per share attributable to common stockholders, basic and diluted(4)	$ (1.45)	$ (1.81)	$ (1.88)	$ (0.42)	$ (0.68)
Weighted-average shares used to compute net loss per share attributable to common stockholders, basic and diluted	57,654	20,974	22,211	21,257	23,495
Pro forma net loss per share, basic and diluted (unaudited)(5)			$ (0.53)		$ (0.20)
Weighted-average shares used in computing pro forma net loss per share, basic and diluted (unaudited)			77,597		78,881

What About The "Accretion" Line Item?

Sometimes investors negotiate terms which provide for the potential redemption of a preferred stock. In those instances, a company can find itself recognizing a charge, in a form similar to that of a dividend, as accretion below its net loss in the income statement.

We care more about the net loss, as it's more closely tied to the company's operating results, instead of this somewhat arcane financial item. But that's what it means, in case you were curious!

You have now gone through an income statement's most basic pieces, giving you the foundations in understanding what it means. The good news for you is that it will never be harder than that. The first run is the worst, as it seems that there's a blizzard of numbers in front of you that you'll never see through.

As an exercise, read the other columns in the income statement. Get a feeling for how the company did in 2016 and 2017, then ask yourself these questions:

- How much did its revenue grow between the two years?
- Was the company less profitable in the first half of 2017 or the first half of 2018?
- Finally, did the company have more cash on hand at the end of 2017 or the end of 2016?

After a few more S-1s, income statements will be nothing to you. Even better, the same income statement notes from above will apply to any earnings report you need to read. That's great!

Finding Quarterly Results

Search for "quarterly results" in the S-1. The third result is what we want. As you can see, we have the company's results broken down by quarter. This lets us see how the firm did during the periods it summarized elsewhere in its filing. You can think of quarterly results as a high form of truth, as the company can't stuff a bad quarter into a year's results to smooth it out.

A few more notes on other things you can find in the S-1 that will be helpful:

- **Finding a company's current cash position.** Run a search on the S-1 page for "cash and," a query that will bring up the data we need. There are 24 results, which is a lot. The good news is that the first one is the correct result (you can find the company's cash position in nearly every S-1 by executing this search or one very similar). Keep in mind that the company's results are presented in thousands. Usually there are two parts: cash and cash equivalents. The combination of the two is generally referred to as simply "cash." Some companies that are very cash-rich will store some of their cash in short-term investments. That counts as cash, too. Apple is so wealthy that it stores some of its cash in long-term investments. Mostly, however, cash in the corporate sense means cash and equivalents.

- **What about stock-based compensation?** After the income statements in this S-1, you'll often see a second table that is preceded by a comment that reads, "Includes stock-based compensation expense as follows." Here the company wants you to know that its net loss isn't as bad as it might appear on a cash basis. As stock-based compensation (paying employees partially in shares) doesn't cost the firm cash, some investors don't count it towards a firm's losses. Companies want you to think that their losses are smaller, so they detail how much of their expenses came from this non-cash cost. You should generally view stock-based compensation as a real cost, as it's mostly a deferred cash cost at best.

Sizing the Offering

You've seen the headline: *Company X Files For $100 Million IPO*. It's often a big, round, precise number that you see in headlines when it comes to new offerings. That number is not accurate.

Companies put placeholder figures in their IPO filings until a price range is set. Regardless, you can get blood from this stone.

Do a search in the S-1 for "Proposed maximum aggregate offering price," which is accountant for "what's the most money you intend to raise?" Here, for example, we see the incredibly common $100 million figure written down. The actual IPO amount will not be $100 million, but will be in the range of $100 million.

Companies that raise $678 million in their IPO don't put $100 million down as a placeholder. They put down $500 million and so forth. Thus, the clean, round placeholder figure is imprecise, but should prove directionally accurate. Just don't ever buy that someone is actually raising $100 million or another nicely rounded number. The chances of it being that exact number are quite small.

Company Details

There are always more numbers to read if you are so inclined, but we need to work out how the company thinks about itself and identify its risks. We'll start with the self-description. Starting on the formal page one of the S-1, the company describes itself in an overview. Next, the company writes about how it thinks about its market ("Industry Background"). Then it usually dives into how it will grow. Following, there is the company's to-be-filled-in offering nuts and bolts (shares, how many, how much, from whom, and so forth). Then the S-1 covers the income statement we know so well.

Risks

It's always worth reading an S-1's risk section. This can tell you about who the company thinks of as competition. It will also note where the firm may run into issues regarding technology and the like.

However, what should not make you worried are boilerplate warnings. To pick one example, every company that goes public and loses money has to say that it may never make money ("We have a history of losses and may not achieve or maintain profitability in the future."). Another classic: "Our future quarterly results of operations are likely to fluctuate significantly due to a wide range of factors, which makes our future results difficult to predict."

This is the company admitting to lacking a crystal ball and the ability to see the future.

However, there are often things of worth in the risk section, so do your homework and skim it. If you don't have that much time, run some searches on the S-1 for keywords that might come up as risks. You'll often find something great.

Every S-1 Is Special

Remember that line about accretion that we dealt with during our income statement work? It's a reminder that every S-1 is special and will require some figuring out. The good news is that Google and the various outcroppings of the Internet (Investopedia, etc.) will help you learn what you don't know. But if you run into something new in an S-1, or something that just plain doesn't make sense, don't worry! Just Google the term and go from there. This is stuff you can figure out. Finance is vocabulary and common sense written down. It's tedious, not difficult; it's opaque, not impossible.

Just keep the basics in mind: revenue up top, real profit on the bottom, and costs in the middle. The harder a company works to make you care less about those things in favor of monthly unique active users divided by fourteen cohorts, the likelier it is that they're full of beans. Also, profit is better than losses in nearly every case.

Lock-Up Period and Hedge Strategies

Quick sellers of post-IPO shares are known as "flippers." Their goal is to make a quick profit, usually selling their shares within a few days of purchase. Your IPO stock shares reside in your brokerage account and you can sell some or all of them at any time.

The process involves placing a sell order online or over the phone, in which you set the price you require and the number of shares to sell. You can place a market order in which you accept the current price or a limit order in which you set a minimum price. You'll receive a notification from your broker when the shares are sold.

The money from the sale, minus commissions and fees, is placed in your brokerage account. As with all shares held for less than one year, any profits you earn from the stock sale are taxed as ordinary income.

Share prices of IPO stock can be highly volatile in the first few days following issuance. The underwriters (investment banks and dealers who distribute IPO shares to subscribers) might artificially support the share price for the first few days. Once the support ends, share prices could plummet. The way to reduce this risk is to sell your shares within a day or two of receiving them. This is a speculative strategy and not always the best one, but there are many restrictions which you must keep in mind.

The underwriters of an IPO generally discourage share flipping because it depresses the post-IPO share prices. That's bad for their future business. To limit flipping, underwriters may refuse to sell IPO shares to customers who have a history of flipping shares. This practice makes it harder for small investors to acquire shares and make quick profits on post-IPO shares.

Keep in mind that if you quickly sell an IPO, you may be penalized by the broker/underwriter that allocated you the shares. The broker usually discloses this in the fine print. Make sure you know your broker's rules before selling your allocation.

Company founders and early investors own private shares of a company before an IPO. If you own private shares, you need to check with the company to see if you are restricted from selling them immediately after the IPO.

Often, private shares are subject to a "lock-up" period of three to six months or longer before they can be sold in the public market. A lock-up might also apply to company employees who receive shares in the IPO. You can check with the issuing company's transfer agent to see if the shares have any restrictions.

A lock-up period is a window of time when investors are not allowed to redeem or sell shares of a particular investment.

- Lock-up periods are when investors cannot sell particular shares or securities.
- Lock-up periods are used to preserve liquidity and maintain market stability.
- Hedge fund managers use them to maintain portfolio stability and liquidity.
- Start-ups/IPOs use them to retain cash and show market resilience.

The lock-up period for newly issued public shares of a company helps stabilize the stock price after it enters the market. When the stock's price and demand are up, the company brings in more money. If business insiders sold their shares to the public, it would appear like the business is not worth investing in and stock prices and demand would go down.

When a privately held company begins the process of going public, key employees may receive reduced cash compensation in exchange for shares of the company's stock. Many of these employees may want to cash in their shares as quickly as possible after the company goes public. The lock-up period prevents stock from being sold immediately after the IPO, when share prices may be artificially high and susceptible to extreme price volatility.

Every possible hedging strategy has been considered and restricted.
However, you do have a few options available to you once the underwriters' lock-up agreement expires after the conclusion of the IPO. I do not recommend you pursue these strategies, but you should be aware that they exist and have an understanding of them. Here they are:

- Short your shares.
- Buy put options on your shares.
- Implement a costless collar.

Short Selling

The simplest way to hedge your position and guarantee your outcome is to *short* your shares. By this we mean borrow shares of your employer's stock from your broker, then sell them in the open market. You then pay back the loan with your exercised options or your RSUs (Restricted Stock Units, a form of stock-based employee compensation) when you are ready. In rare cases, shorting your employer's stock is prohibited by your stock option or RSU agreement. Please make sure you check your agreement, should you wish to pursue this strategy. Brokers charge interest on the borrowed shares, ranging from 0% to in excess of 40% annually depending on how many shares trade each week and the total number of shares that have already been shorted. The greater the liquidity, the lower the interest rate. The more shares that have been shorted, the higher the rate. For example, the current annual rate to short Facebook shares is only 0.5%, while the current rate to short Twitter shares is currently 10-13%, but can be as high as 44%. In some cases, it may not even be possible to find shares to short.

When you short shares, you must keep collateral in your account equal to the number of shares borrowed multiplied by the current price to ensure you can afford to buy back the shares in the open market and close out your short position. Keep in mind that this can represent a very significant additional investment and may be impractical or too risky. If the shares shorted increase in value, you must add to the collateral held in your account. Collateral must be in the form of cash or freely tradable securities, so you can't use stock options or RSUs that haven't yet vested.

The need to maintain collateral makes it very unattractive to short highly volatile stocks, like the ones that have recently been released from their underwriting lock-up restrictions. In fact, in some cases a run-up in a stock can become self-fulfilling as short-sellers, unable to meet the capital call, are then forced to buy back the stock at the new, higher price, spiking demand in the process. This is known as a *short squeeze*.

Prior to 1997, there was a tremendous tax benefit in using a short sale to hedge your position. You could lock in a sale price using shorted shares, then close out the short one year after you originally exercised your options to create a long-term capital gain. This was known in the trade as a *short against the box*. Unfortunately, the IRS changed the rules in 1997, such that the capital gains clock no longer runs while you have a short against the box, which eliminated the tax benefit to shorting. You might as well just sell your shares if you want to lock in a price. This avoids interest costs and the need to maintain collateral in your brokerage account.

Put Options

Another way to hedge a position is to buy *put options* to protect your downside risk. A put option is **a right to sell your stock** at a predetermined price in the future. In this case, you might want to buy an option to sell your stock at something that approximates what you consider the current fair (or high) price.

The more volatile the stock and higher the price at which you want to sell, the higher the cost of the put option. For example, Facebook's closing price on March 14, 2014, was $67.72 per share. A put option to sell Facebook at $67.50 over the next three months would cost $6.90 per share, whereas an alternative put option to sell Facebook at $52.50 (approximately 20% below the current price) over the next three months' costs only $1.51 per share, but provides less protection.

There are a number of factors that affect the price of option contracts, but volatility is one of them. Put options in Facebook are relatively expensive as a percentage of its stock price because Facebook is such a volatile stock.

The commissions to purchase or sell options tend to cost approximately 1 to 3 cents per share. Some brokers charge 1.5 cents per share for options priced below $1 per share, while it's 3 cents per share for all options priced higher than $1 per share. Option contracts are only sold for round lots of 100 shares. There is no fee or commission for expiring contracts. However, standard commissions are charged on the sale of your stock when it is ultimately sold.

In a way, put options can be thought of as insurance. You are paying a price up front for a guarantee that you can sell at a given price, if you want or need to. Your best-case outcome, should you pursue this strategy, is the current price of your stock minus the cost of the put option minus the commission on the put option. In our Facebook example, you would net $60.79 ($67.72 – $6.90 – $0.03) if you chose to buy put options at the current price. As you can see, it can cost more than 10% of the value of your holdings to hedge your position in this way.

The Costless Collar

A collar, commonly known as a hedge wrapper, is an options strategy implemented to protect against large losses. However, it also limits large gains. An investor creates a collar position by purchasing an out-of-the-money put option while simultaneously writing an out-of-the-money call option. The put protects the trader in case the price of the stock drops. Writing the call produces income (which should ideally offset the cost of buying the put) and allows the trader to profit on the stock up to the strike price of the call, but not higher.

For some people, the prospect of trading some of their potential upside gain for a guarantee to limit their downside is appealing. The most popular way to address the great expense of purchasing a put option is to implement a *costless collar*, which means you simultaneously sell a call option on your stock when you buy your put option. A call option is the opposite of a put option; it entitles you to *buy* a stock at a predetermined price up until a particular time in the future. Selling the call option gives you the money to buy the put option, hence the term *costless*.

In our previous example, a put option to sell Facebook over the next three months at $52.50 (down approximately 20%) costs us $1.51 per share. A call option to buy Facebook at $85.00 for the next three months would net us $1.69 per share. We could finance the purchase of the put option with the sale of call options. Keep in mind that we would pay 3 cents per share for each put and call option, so the profit would be very small. With this collar in place, we don't have to worry about our stock going down by up to 22.5% ($67.72 to $52.50), but we will not be able to hold on to our stock if it rises above $85.00 per share.

It doesn't make sense to buy put options and sell call options at the current trading price of your stock because it would lock you into selling at the current price, which would be much less expensive to accomplish than if you just sold your stock directly.

Most institutional investors prefer not to implement the costless collar because of the high cost of the options commissions and how it limits their upside.

Conclusion

Shorting stock and trading options are activities that should be limited to people who have experience with those strategies. Furthermore, our discussion of using these approaches to *hedge* in no way condones their use as *trading strategies* to make a profit. In theory, hedging your hard-earned stock options and RSUs can make a lot of sense.

Unfortunately, there simply aren't any really good options to do so, which might just make selling a chunk of your stock upfront and the remainder over time a much better strategy.

This means the largest shareholders in the business can only freely sell their shares after the IPO lock-up expiration. A flood of new shares can come onto the market if the owners of those shares decide to sell. If the share price has soared since the IPO, then early investors may want to reap the rewards by selling some of their investments.

Or, if the price has tanked, then they may look to reduce their exposure. However, it doesn't mean they will sell either way, as they could look to retain shares in the hopes of prices heading even higher, or because they believe shares could recover any value lost in the early days as a public company.

A lot of attention is paid to how the share price has performed versus the IPO price, but it is worth remembering that early investors are likely to have paid significantly less. This means many early investors will still be able to book a profit even if the share price has performed poorly after the IPO.

The end of a lock-up period sends a strong signal about the confidence the largest shareholders have in the company's prospects. If institutional investors decide to dump the stock once the lock-up period ends, then this suggests they have little faith that the company is worth holding. If a relatively small number of shares are sold by these investors, then this shows they want to retain the shares and are bullish on the stock's prospects.

Typically, if there is a sharp increase in the number of shares available in a company, then this pushes the price of a stock down. It is not unusual to see a stock's share price fall on the first day that the lock-up shares can be traded. In fact, if other investors (not subject to the lock-up period) begin to sell in the days before the lock-up expires, then this is a sign that they expect the share price to fall.

However, there is also an argument that the end of a lock-up period can provide support after any immediate sell-off. This is because it also means there is increased liquidity in the stock – which financial institutions and large investors like. Liquidity can be restrained during the lock-up period because it is not uncommon for the majority of a stock's shares to be subject to it, which could mean they don't initially meet the criteria demanded by the likes of institutions or pension funds.

How to forecast the effect of a lock-up period expiring on the share price:

- **How does the share price perform in the days before the lock-up period expires?** This usually shows how other investors expect the expiration of the lock-up period to impact the share price.

- **How has the share price performed since the IPO?** If shares have rallied since listing, this could entice investors to sell shares once the lock-up period expires. If it has tanked, this could discourage them from selling but could also entice them to reduce their exposure and cut some of their losses. Remember, their entry point will be lower than the IPO price, so they can still sell at a profit even if the share price has performed badly since listing.

- **How is the business performing?** Many of this year's largest IPOs have been companies that have questionable business models, such as Uber, which has confessed it may never be profitable. In the current climate where uncertainty reigns supreme, investors are looking for safer bets and have less of an appetite for riskier investments like high-growth but unprofitable businesses. This could encourage a larger sell-off once the lock-up period expires, as investors look to redeploy their cash to safer alternatives. Remember, lock-up investors have not been able to respond to any news since the IPO.

- **How many shares are subject to the lock-up period?** The number of shares subject to a lock-up is usually quite large. The more of a company's share capital that is subject to the lock-up period, the greater the potential selling pressure will be.

- **Who owns the shares subject to the lock-up period?** Understanding who owns the shares subject to the lock-up can provide further insight as to whether they will look to sell their stake when it expires. Consider the strategy behind each shareholder's stake and why they own it. For example, if the majority of lock-up shares are owned by founders and management, then they are less likely to sell large stakes compared to institutions or funds that have invested early on. If employees have been paid in shares, then they will cash in at the first opportunity.

How to choose the best brokerage service?

The broker is the bridge between the investor and the market. All ordinary investors who want to invest money in IPOs need to use a broker's services to access the market. Accessing the market is the first step before starting to invest.

Before opening any brokerage account, always weigh the pros and cons of the broker firm. You must be fully aware of all commissions, limits, and restrictions. However, first of all, the broker must be suitable for you and your strategy, not vice versa.

No brokerage firm can guarantee you will be able to purchase shares in an initial public offering (IPO).
While it can be difficult for individual investors to buy IPO shares, more firms, including several online brokers, offer IPOs. Because these firms often have a small allotment of shares to sell to the public, your ability to buy these shares – especially "hot" IPOs – may be limited, no matter with which firm you do business.

Brokerage firms may also sell shares in the IPO only to selected clients. For example, some firms limit sales of shares in an IPO to those customers who have certain cash balances in their accounts, are active traders with the firm, or subscribe to one of their more expensive "premium" services. In addition, some firms impose restrictions on investors who "flip" or sell their IPO shares soon after trading in the shares to make a quick profit. If you flip your IPO shares, your firm may refuse to sell you any other IPOs or prevent you from buying an IPO for several months. Brokerage firms often list these restrictions on the firm's website.
The best brokerages give IPO access to all US based investors that have an account, regardless of the amount of assets in the account. The worst require high account balances for existing wealthy customers or have no access to IPOs at all.

In recent years, a new group of brokerages has emerged that allow access to IPOs for anyone with an account, regardless of account balance. Instead of rewarding wealthy customers, they are using the IPO opportunity to gain new customers. Companies are now using the IPO as a way to build loyalty with the customer, who is more likely to buy products from them as shareholders.

This new idea of connecting the customer by allowing access to the IPO is just getting started. IPO investing is the trend of recent years. As new companies see the benefits, more will follow suit, opening up further opportunities for IPO investors. However, then there is allocation. With more people starting to invest in IPO, allocation is worsening.

Let's take a look at some US online brokers which offer access to IPOs, including their limits and restrictions.

Brokers Overview:

Most of the big discount brokers – TD Ameritrade, Fidelity, Charles Schwab, and E*Trade, for example – offer access to at least some IPOs. Each imposes different requirements for participation, but in every case you must have an account with a broker in order to invest in an IPO via that broker.

Prove eligibility
TD Ameritrade will permit you to invest in an IPO if you have at least $250,000 in assets with the firm *or* have traded stock with Ameritrade at least 30 times in the last 12 months. In this way, Ameritrade is limiting IPO access to what it considers its better customers.

Fidelity's requirements are similar. Customers who have $100,000 with the broker are eligible to participate in IPOs led by underwriter **Kohlberg Kravis Roberts (KKR)**. Fidelity limits participation to customers with $500,000 and those who have placed 36 trades in the past year.

Schwab's requirements are easier to meet: $100,000 in your account or 36 trades in your history.

E*Trade has no brokerage account minimum, but requires you to fill out a questionnaire from the underwriters.

Access to IPOs through TradeStation broker.

In the past, it's been nearly impossible for retail traders to access initial public offerings (IPOs) before the shares become available on the exchanges.

TradeStation clients now have access to certain ground-floor initial public offerings (IPOs), secondary offerings, and follow-on offerings available in the mobile-first **ClickIPO app.**
- Clients can easily browse IPOs and view the price range, anticipated offering date, SEC prospectus, and more.
- Simply place a conditional order for shares through a TradeStation account and, if shares are allocated, they will be placed directly into your account.

Features of ClickIPO
ClickIPO is a mobile-based order entry platform that gives retail investors access to IPOs and secondary offerings. All you need is a TradeStation equities brokerage account with a minimum balance of $500, then you're ready to get started.
Pricing and Funding
- When you purchase IPO stock in your TradeStation account using ClickIPO, there's no commission on the trade. If the stock is priced at $10 per share, you'll pay $10 per share – no more, no less.
- IPO stock cannot be purchased using margin. You must have sufficient unrestricted cash in your account to pay for your IPO shares.

IPO Alternatives

The IPO has been around since the dawn of the stock markets, but after a peak of more than 300 IPOs a year in the 90s, we've seen close to 100 IPOs per year, on average, over the past two decades. Part of that is due to regulatory changes that allowed companies to have a larger number of private shareholders (up to nearly 2,000) and privately raise larger rounds of capital (upwards of $500 million to $1 billion) without being forced to go public.

With an IPO, a company steps through a series of hoops that can last from several months to years. A company typically hires an investment bank to guide it through the process in exchange for a fee of about 4–7 percent of the money raised. That includes helping the company prepare an S-1 (a prospectus required by the SEC that provides a deep dive into the company's financials, future plans, and its team) and lining up a one- to two-month-long roadshow to pitch investors on the company. Those investor meetings gauge investor demand and help bankers determine an offering share price.

IPOs are expensive and time consuming. On average, companies spend $750,000 and 18 months preparing for an IPO. There have long been complaints from companies about underpricing, when an underwriter prices shares too cheaply, leading to a big opening day pop but less money raised for the company.

So let's take a look at alternative ways for companies to go public, raise capital, and sell their shares publicly.

Reverse Merger or SPAC

Call this the sneaky way to become a public company. Essentially, a private company takes control and merges with a public company, often a dormant shell corporation that doesn't have assets or real operations, but does have a ticker symbol.
Reverse mergers were popular 30 to 40 years ago and hundreds of companies sought out "zombie" shells to trade on the public markets. In the 1980s, they were a favorite among small natural resource companies.

Over the past decade, the SEC has cracked down on the practice after several reverse-merger companies — including some foreign firms that used the practice to enter U.S. markets — were accused of "pump and dump" schemes to scam investors. In 2011, the SEC issued a fraud warning, urging caution when investing in companies that went public through reverse mergers. Over the next few years, the agency suspended trading for more than 800 shell companies.

What Is a Special Purpose Acquisition Company (SPAC)?
A special purpose acquisition company (SPAC) is a company with no commercial operations that is formed strictly to raise capital through an initial public offering (IPO) for the purpose of acquiring an existing company. They are also known as "blank check companies" or "shell companies". They've become more popular in recent years, attracting big-name underwriters and investors and raising a record amount of IPO money in 2019. In 2020, as of the beginning of August, more than 50 SPACs have been formed in the U.S. which have raised some $21.5 billion.

How a SPAC Works?

SPACs are generally formed by investors or sponsors with expertise in a particular industry or business sector, with the intention of pursuing deals in that area. In creating a SPAC, the founders sometimes have at least one acquisition target in mind, but they don't identify that target to avoid extensive disclosures during the IPO process. This is why they are called "blank check companies." IPO investors have no idea in which company they will ultimately be investing.) SPACs seek underwriters and institutional investors before offering shares to the public.

The money SPACs raise in an IPO is placed in an interest-bearing trust account. These funds cannot be disbursed except to complete an acquisition or to return the money to investors if the SPAC is liquidated. A SPAC generally has two years to complete a deal or face liquidation. In some cases, some of the interest earned from the trust can be used as the SPAC's working capital. After an acquisition, a SPAC is usually listed on one of the major stock exchanges.

Advantages of a SPAC

Selling to a SPAC can be an attractive option for the owners of a smaller company, which are often private equity funds. First, selling to a SPAC can add up to 20% to the sale price compared to a typical private equity deal. Being acquired by a SPAC can also offer business owners what is essentially a faster IPO process under the guidance of an experienced partner, with less worry about the swings in broader market sentiments.

SPACs Make a Comeback

The SPAC craze of 2020 has shown no signs of slowing down, as more and more companies sidestep the traditional IPO process in favor of a faster and cheaper path to public markets.

219 SPACs have raised $73 billion in proceeds, representing a year-over-year jump of 462% and outpacing traditional IPOs by $6 billion, according to a note from Goldman Sachs.

Examples of High-Profile SPAC Deals

One of the most high-profile recent deals involving special purpose acquisition companies involved Richard Branson's Virgin Galactic. Venture capitalist Chamath Palihapitiya's SPAC Social Capital Hedosophia Holdings bought a 49% stake in Virgin Galactic for $800 million before listing the company in 2019.

In 2020, Bill Ackman (founder of Pershing Square Capital Management) sponsored his own SPAC, Pershing Square Tontine Holdings, the largest-ever SPAC which raised $4 billion in its offering on July 22.

Direct Listing

The direct listing is the IPO alternative. It lets the company avoid many of the headaches of an IPO and go public without issuing new shares. Instead, you sell a small amount of existing shares directly to the public once listed on an exchange. Unlike an IPO, a company doesn't raise new capital. However, a lot of today's tech startups are already well capitalized thanks to the big dollars in private markets.

A number of investors, including venture capitalist Bill Gurley of Benchmark Capital, have become outspoken proponents of direct listings because they see today's investment banking models as inefficient and outdated. They want an efficient way for early investors to sell some of their stakes without padding the pockets of investment banks. Slack and Spotify both went public using direct listings.

A direct public offering (DPO) is a type of offering in which a company offers its securities directly to the public to raise capital. An issuing company using a DPO eliminates the intermediaries – investment banks, broker-dealers, and underwriters – that are typical in initial public offerings (IPO). Instead, it self-underwrites its securities.

Cutting out the intermediaries from a public offering substantially lowers the cost of capital of a DPO. Therefore, a DPO is attractive to small companies and companies with an established and loyal client base. A DPO is also known as direct placement.

How a Direct Public Offering Works

When a firm issues securities through a direct public offering (DPO), it raises money independently without the restrictions associated with bank and venture capital financing. The terms of the offering are solely up to the issuer, who guides and tailors the process according to the company's best interests. The issuer sets the offering price, the minimum investment per investor, the limit on the number of securities that any one investor can buy, the settlement date, and the offering period within which investors can purchase the securities and after which the offering will be closed.

On December 22, 2020, the U.S. Securities and Exchange Commission announced that it will allow companies to raise capital through direct listings, paving the way for circumvention of the traditional initial public offering (IPO) process. In addition to saving on fees, companies that follow the direct listing process may avoid the usual IPO restrictions, including lock-up periods that prevent insiders from selling their shares for a defined period of time.

IPO ETF and mutual funds

If you're a beginner in IPO Investing, you should assume ETF (exchange-traded funds) for your investing strategy, or at least diversify your IPO portfolio with exchange traded funds.

IPO ETFs have a range of IPOs, from those with the greatest values to those who went public in the last year. Each ETF has its own rules about which companies are listed and for how long. In addition, IPO ETFs can be found under equity and fixed income asset classes.
IPO investing is a popular and exciting market. However, a company's IPO can also be risky. That's why some investors recommend IPO ETFs; they provide a diversified portfolio of IPOs. This can decrease risk while giving investors exposure to recent and sometimes top IPOs. For example, Renaissance Capital's IPO ETF (IPO) was one of the most popular and high growth ETFs.

IPO ETFs invest in the equity of companies that have recently had their initial public offerings. The first IPO ETF was the First Trust US IPO Index ETF (FPX), which was launched in 2006. Although these ETFs seek to capitalize on the growth and innovation of new companies, they do not offer access to pre-IPO equity.

With 8 ETFs traded on the U.S. markets, IPO ETFs have total assets under management of $4.62B. The average expense ratio is 0.57%. IPO ETFs can be found in the following asset classes:
- Equity
- Fixed Income

The largest IPO ETF is the First Trust U.S. Equity Opportunities ETF FPX with $2.23B in assets. In the last trailing year, the best-performing IPO ETF was IPO at 119.32%. The most recent ETF launched in the IPO space was the Defiance Next Gen SPAC Derived ETF SPAK on September 30th, 2020.

Below is a description of each ETF, including issuer and expense ratio.
I'll mention 7 ETFs because Goldman Sachs Access Inflation Protected USD Bond ETF (GTIP) is mostly concentrated on bonds and only rare IPOs.

First Trust U.S. Equity Opportunities ETF (FPX)
Issuer: First Trust
Expense Ratio: 0.58%
Inception Date: April 12, 2006

FPX tracks the 100 largest U.S. IPOs. It's determined by market-cap and the ETF holds the stock for the first 1,000 days of trading. That's roughly a four-year period. Its requirements include:

- Minimum market cap of $50 million at close of first trading day
- Publicly traded float of 15% minimum
- No abnormal pricing (defined as three standard deviations greater than the mean)

PERFORMANCE [as of 02/16/21]	1 MONTH	3 MONTHS	YTD	1 YEAR	3 YEARS	5 YEARS	10 YEARS
FPX	7.18%	31.08%	14.94%	58.33%	25.87%	26.45%	19.46%
FPX (NAV)	8.87%	29.71%	14.28%	56.49%	24.56%	25.68%	19.30%
IPOX-100 U.S. Index	--	--	--	--	--	--	--
MSCI USA IMI	4.90%	11.87%	6.18%	22.65%	16.11%	18.86%	13.83%

Source: etf.com

Invesco S&P Spin-Off ETF (CSD)
Issuer: Invesco
Expense Ratio: 0.62%
Inception Date: December 15, 2006

CSD tracks large- and mid-cap U.S. equities that became independent of their parent company in the last four years. This mostly applies to company spin-offs, which tend to be more focused on its core business or product rather than the company as a whole. For example, SpaceX's spinoff Starlink. This IPO ETF reconstitutes on a monthly basis. At that time, companies are able to immediately list in the ETF. A single company has a cap of 7% CSD also has a $1 billion market cap minimum.

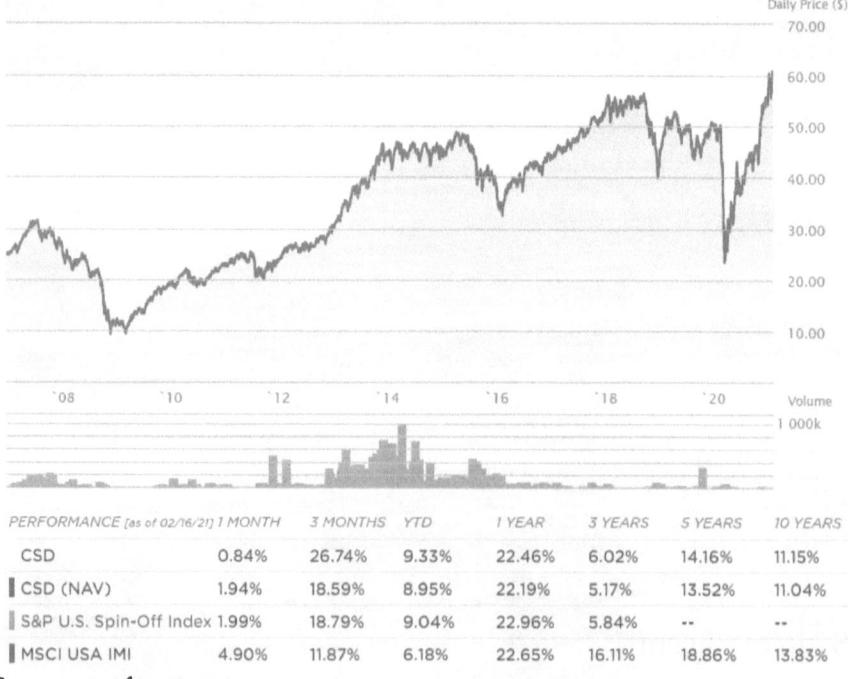

PERFORMANCE [as of 02/16/21]	1 MONTH	3 MONTHS	YTD	1 YEAR	3 YEARS	5 YEARS	10 YEARS
CSD	0.84%	26.74%	9.33%	22.46%	6.02%	14.16%	11.15%
CSD (NAV)	1.94%	18.59%	8.95%	22.19%	5.17%	13.52%	11.04%
S&P U.S. Spin-Off Index	1.99%	18.79%	9.04%	22.96%	5.84%	--	--
MSCI USA IMI	4.90%	11.87%	6.18%	22.65%	16.11%	18.86%	13.83%

Source: etf.com

Renaissance IPO ETF (IPO)
Issuer: Renaissance Capital
Expense Ratio: 0.12%
Inception Date: October 14, 2013
IPO tracks the newest listings on the U.S. markets. It adds IPOs within 90 days of listing and keeps them for two years. The largest IPOs can be added within a week of listing. Companies have a 10% issuer cap and are reviewed quarterly. This limits the weight of any company listed in the ETF.

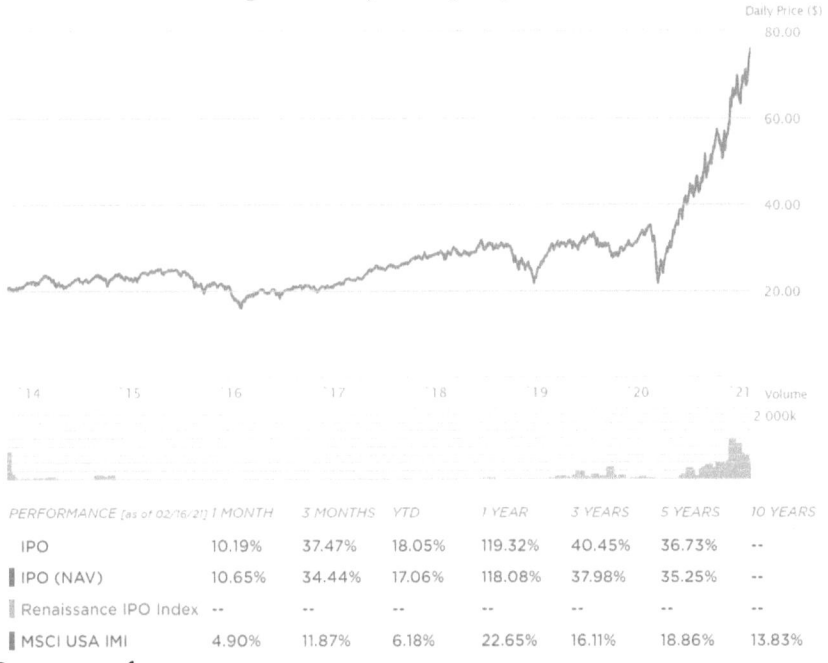

PERFORMANCE [as of 02/16/21]	1 MONTH	3 MONTHS	YTD	1 YEAR	3 YEARS	5 YEARS	10 YEARS
IPO	10.19%	37.47%	18.05%	119.32%	40.45%	36.73%	--
IPO (NAV)	10.65%	34.44%	17.06%	118.08%	37.98%	35.25%	--
Renaissance IPO Index	--	--	--	--	--	--	--
MSCI USA IMI	4.90%	11.87%	6.18%	22.65%	16.11%	18.86%	13.83%

Source: etf.com

Renaissance International IPO ETF (IPOS)
Issuer: Renaissance Capital
Expense Ratio: 0.8%
Inception Date: October 6, 2014

IPOS is Renaissance Capital's international ETF. Similar to its sister IPO ETF, it adds companies within 90 days of listing. The fund keeps a company for only two years.
However, the IPOS ETF doesn't include international companies that list on a U.S. exchange. Instead, these companies are listed in Renaissance's other ETF, IPO. IPOS focuses on small-growth firms and its expense ratio is considered high for a cap-weighted ETF.

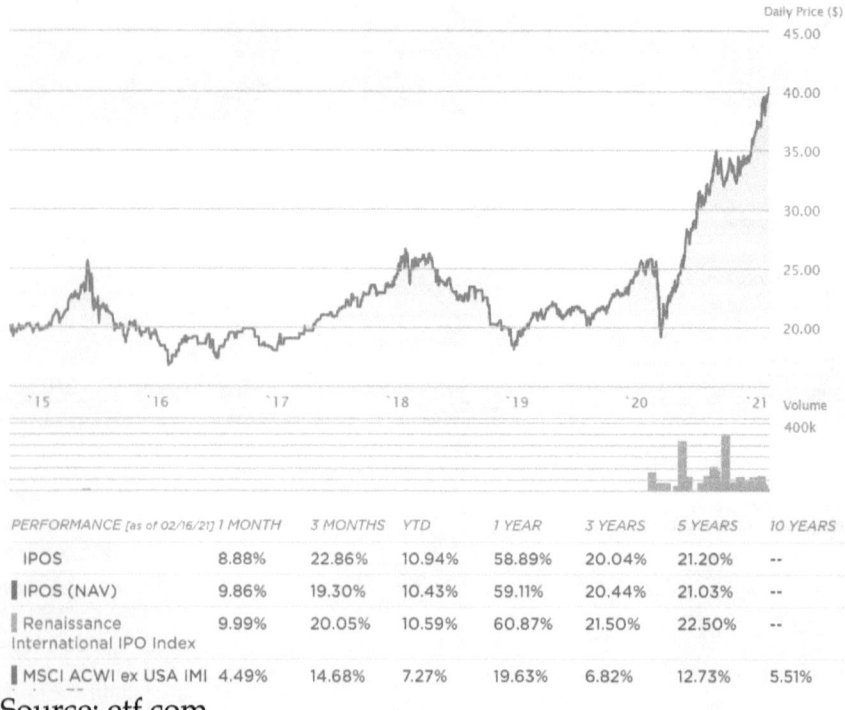

PERFORMANCE [as of 02/16/21]	1 MONTH	3 MONTHS	YTD	1 YEAR	3 YEARS	5 YEARS	10 YEARS
IPOS	8.88%	22.86%	10.94%	58.89%	20.04%	21.20%	--
IPOS (NAV)	9.86%	19.30%	10.43%	59.11%	20.44%	21.03%	--
Renaissance International IPO Index	9.99%	20.05%	10.59%	60.87%	21.50%	22.50%	--
MSCI ACWI ex USA IMI	4.49%	14.68%	7.27%	19.63%	6.82%	12.73%	5.51%

Source: etf.com

First Trust International Equity Opportunities ETF (FPXI)
Issuer: First Trust
Expense Ratio: 0.7%
Inception Date: Inception Date: November 5, 2014

FPXI holds 50 of the largest international companies who recently went public. Companies can be added on the sixth day of trading. They are held for 1,000 days or roughly four years. Requirements for the FPXI ETF include:
- Minimum market cap of $50 million at close of first trading day
- Publicly traded float of 15% minimum
- No abnormal pricing (defined as three standard deviations greater than the mean)

This IPO ETF also has a 10% issuer cap in place and is rebalanced quarterly. This can lead to big changes as new firms enter and old ones exit.

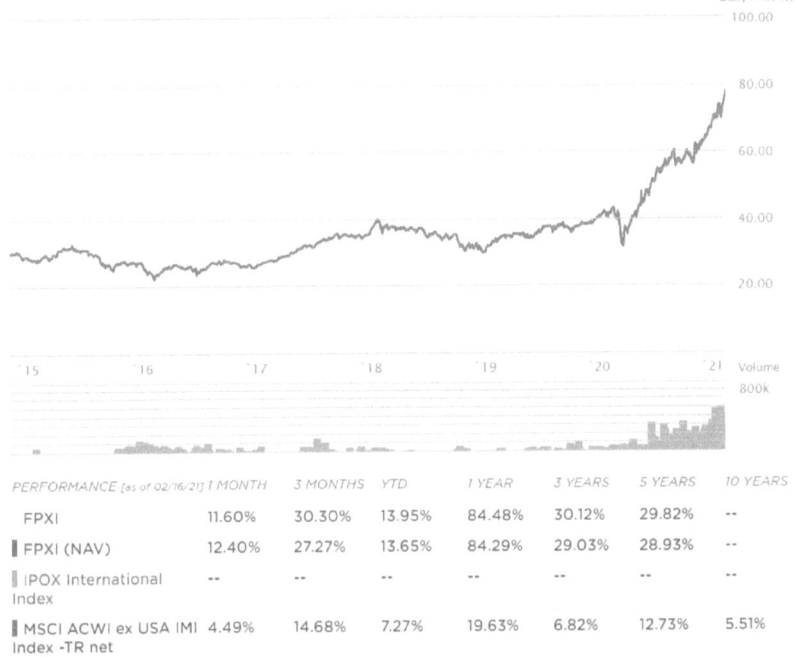

PERFORMANCE [as of 02/16/21]	1 MONTH	3 MONTHS	YTD	1 YEAR	3 YEARS	5 YEARS	10 YEARS
FPXI	11.60%	30.30%	13.95%	84.48%	30.12%	29.82%	--
FPXI (NAV)	12.40%	27.27%	13.65%	84.29%	29.03%	28.93%	--
IPOX International Index	--	--	--	--	--	--	--
MSCI ACWI ex USA IMI Index -TR net	4.49%	14.68%	7.27%	19.63%	6.82%	12.73%	5.51%

Source: etf.com

First Trust IPOX Europe Equity Opportunities ETF (FPXE)
Issuer: First Trust
Expense Ratio: 0.7%
Inception Date: October 4, 2018

FPXE holds positions in the Stocks are purchased on the sixth day of trading. They're held for 1,000 days or roughly four years. This IPO ETF's requirements include:
- Minimum market cap of $50 million at close of first trading day
- Publicly traded float of 15% minimum
- No abnormal pricing (defined as three standard deviations greater than the mean)

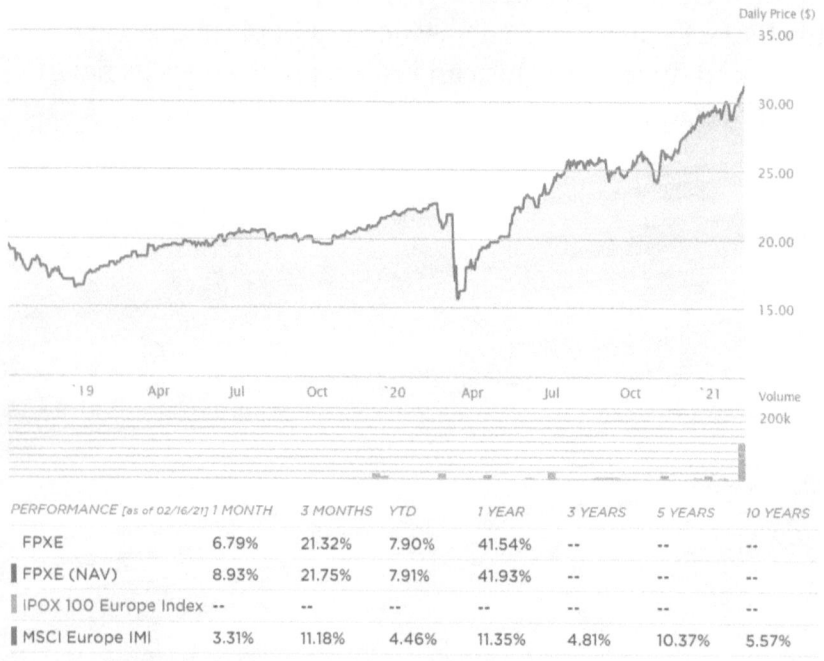

PERFORMANCE [as of 02/16/21]	1 MONTH	3 MONTHS	YTD	1 YEAR	3 YEARS	5 YEARS	10 YEARS
FPXE	6.79%	21.32%	7.90%	41.54%	--	--	--
FPXE (NAV)	8.93%	21.75%	7.91%	41.93%	--	--	--
IPOX 100 Europe Index	--	--	--	--	--	--	--
MSCI Europe IMI	3.31%	11.18%	4.46%	11.35%	4.81%	10.37%	5.57%

Source: etf.com

Defiance NextGen SPAC Derived ETF (SPAK)
Issuer: Defiance
Expense Ratio: 0.45%
Inception Date: September 30, 2020

SPAK is a new IPO ETF. It tracks U.S.-listed special purpose acquisition companies (SPACs) and SPAC-derived companies. It's the first ETF of its kind, as SPAC IPOs became popular in recent years, particularly 2020.

This ETF will be rebalanced on an annual basis in July. SPAK is weighted 80% SPAC-derived companies and 20% SPACs. New SPACs meeting requirements can be added quarterly, whereas SPAC-derived companies can be added monthly.

PERFORMANCE [as of 02/16/21]	1 MONTH	3 MONTHS	YTD	1 YEAR	3 YEARS	5 YEARS	10 YEARS
SPAK	14.37%	41.33%	19.80%	--	--	--	--
SPAK (NAV)	15.94%	39.63%	21.81%	--	--	--	--
Indxx SPAC & NextGen IPO Index	--	--	--	--	--	--	--
MSCI USA IMI	4.90%	11.87%	6.18%	22.65%	16.11%	18.86%	13.83%

Source: etf.com

Risks of IPO investing

By its nature, investing in an IPO is a risky and speculative investment. Brokerage firms must consider whether the IPO is appropriate for you in light of your income and net worth, investment objectives, other securities holdings, risk tolerance, and other factors. A firm may not sell IPO shares to you unless it has determined the investment is suitable for you.

Smaller investors still need to weigh the pros and cons before buying an IPO. As the time-honored adage goes, buyer beware. IPO purchases are not without risk, which can be significant at times.

And while the first-day pop of an IPO is legendary, that doesn't mean that the future will work out as merrily. Consider that some of the highest-flying IPOs of recent times have lost their luster with Wall Street investors after an initial honeymoon.

Snap, Twitter, Spotify, and even Facebook all fell substantially after their stocks debuted. Of this group, only Facebook has managed to surpass its IPO price on a consistent basis.

Also, the discount offered at the initial public offering is generally not that great. According to Shelton Smith, the IPO price should be, on average, a 13-15 percent discount from what the regular trading price might be once the stock is public.

If you're considering buying an IPO, you'll need to research and evaluate the company's business model. You'll look to assess its future plans and want to see whether the company is consistently profitable – or at least has a path to consistent profitability.

Amazingly, many companies come to market without a clear plan to generate sustained profits.

New IPOs often have limited histories, so they can be tough to assess and value. This is particularly true when a company is in a nascent industry, as dotcom companies were in the 1990s and social media, ride-sharing, and electronic payment companies are today.

To get some insight into how the company works and how the stock is valued, investors can look at the massive registration document required by the Securities and Exchange Commission for all new securities.

Known as Form S-1, or the Registration Statement Under the Securities Exchange Act of 1933, the offering document must contain specific information for investors, including financial information, the business model, risk factors, and information about the industry. This document can be found on the SEC's website and is normally loaded with caveats and disclaimers. If investors can wade through the document, they can glean enough information about the new company to make a call about the valuation — is it worth buying at the price people are selling?

Buying IPO stocks requires a lot of homework and they can be risky.

Even for those who are able to get in on the first-day pop, IPOs may not be a sure bet. Thus, most individual investors should consider new companies carefully. It's wise to limit your position size on any individual stock to a few percent of your holdings.

CONCLUSION

Dear readers, you are now sufficiently familiar with the IPO stocks investing process.

I hope that "IPO Investing Guide" will help you to profitably and wisely invest your money, meaning you become freer and more financially independent.
I've spent a lot of time in my life helping people find their passion and build a wealthy future, where everyone can live the life they desire.

Thank you for reading my book! This is the second book in the Investing series.

I believe that you will have found the information in this guide useful and have taken one step forward in your plan to achieve success in your life.

As an indie author, your opinion regarding this book is VERY IMPORTANT to me, not to mention its influence on your future decisions.

Thus, I'd be delighted to see your honest review on Amazon.

I read and take them all into consideration for future improvements in my writing skills and ability to transfer the most important information to you, my dear reader!

Thank you for your time and decision to read my book!
Sign up to my social media to become the first to receive information regarding new books released in the Investing series.

IPO Investing Guide

www.ingramcontent.com/pod-product-compliance
Lightning Source LLC
Chambersburg PA
CBHW030444220526
45464CB00006B/2409